UNCOMMON
LEADERSHIP

ADVANCE PRAISE FOR
UNCOMMON LEADERSHIP

"I was excited to dive into Ben's new book *Uncommon Leadership*, and it definitely did not disappoint! Ben Newman is one of the most genuine and powerful people I have come across, and his chapters highlighting others with similar qualities left me feeling inspired, rejuvenated, and ready to tackle anything life throws at me. Thank you, Ben, for continuing to shine your light. It radiates brightly, and your mom would be SO proud."

—Rebekah Gregory | Founder & CEO of Rebekah's Angels Foundation Inspirational Speaker & Author Boston Marathon Bombing Survivor

"Ben Newman consistently is helping those who are already considered at the top of their game. The difference between those who are known and unknown are the ones who are willing to do the small things every damn day! The gems that you take away from one of Ben's talks, a moment, an exchange, and now he leaves us *Uncommon Leadership*. Helping everyone who reads it get those gems that help you elevate your game! You will not be disappointed!"

—Michael Kennedy Jr | CEO, KAI Enterprises

"The qualities of those who possess mental toughness and achieve greatness in life are abnormal and uncommon. Ben Newman's fire and passion show you how to go beyond what's common to own your success."

—Dr. Ellen Reed | Best-selling author, performance coach, speaker

"I learned while at Alabama that you have Prizefighter Days. When stacking PrizeFighter days, you develop the uncommon mindset. You prepare to attack the field and you take an uncommon mindset to the game. You see, high levels of success are uncommon. Sustaining them is even more uncommon. Prizefighter Days prepare you to attack the big goals that you create which allows you to reach peak performance."'"

—Mac Jones | 2x National Champion with Alabama Football, Davey O'Brien Award Winner & Heisman Finalist, New England Patriots Quarterback

"This book is a must-read for all leaders. Ben lays out a formula for success for all types of leaders with his stories of 11 distinct leadership styles from some of the most accomplished people in their respective fields, and then he brings it all together in a way only Ben can. No matter the leadership style one chooses, you must have 100% commitment. This book re-energized me to be ALL IN on my leadership journey."

—Rob Lee | Executive Vice President,
Wanzek Construction, Inc.

"I have studied the highest level of performance my entire career. The highest performers show up differently every day. They are RELENTLESS. They are UNCOMMON. If you want to better understand the mindset of high performers, *Uncommon Leadership* will help unlock what it takes. Then it's your choice."

—Dr. Jason Selk | Founder, Enhanced Performance, Inc., Former Director of Sport Psychology for the St. Louis Cardinals

"*Uncommon Leadership* is mandatory reading for anyone currently in a leadership position and those who hope to be! The stories that Ben has compiled from some of the most impressive elite performers and high achievers of our lifetime are invaluable. Ben has a passion that is always burning, and that passion is shared in the stories contained in these pages. If you want to become a better version of yourself, read this book, write your I AM statements, and GET TO WORK!"

—Ted Rath | Vice President of Player Performance, Philadelphia Eagles

UNCOMMON LEADERSHIP

11 WAYS THE GREATEST LEADERS LEAD

BEN NEWMAN

Cataloging-in-Publication data is available.

ISBN 13: 978-1-954020-05-4 (Hardback)
ISBN 13: 978-1-954020-06-1 (Ebook)

10 9 8 7 6 5 4 3 2 1

First Edition

Dedicated to my wife, Ami, and our children, J. Isaac and Kennedy Rose. My mother—your grandmother—taught me the profound lesson of LEGACY. It is now our responsibility to show you how to fight for yours each and every day.

In loving memory of Janet Fishman Newman.

"When your mind is telling you that you're done, that you're exhausted, that you cannot possibly go any farther, you're actually only 40% done."

—David Goggins, *Can't Hurt Me*

TABLE OF CONTENTS

FOREWORD

BY ED MYLETT
CEO, #MAXOUT

I f you know anything about Ben Newman, it should come as no surprise my friend has written *Uncommon Leadership*. That's because he doesn't just sermonize about uncommon leadership. Ben lives uncommon leadership, just like the people he writes about in this book. How so? His mission in life is to help lead the leaders.

Ben is real. What you see is what you get. There are no hidden agendas, no tricks, no mind games or magic acts.

Ben is disciplined, yet he holds nothing back. I have rarely met a man or a woman with Ben's level of passion. In a world where so many people are afraid to commit their entire being to what they believe in, Ben is uncommon because he never flinches. He is fully immersed in his thoughts and deeds.

Ben is fearless. He never wavers, and he is relentless in studying what it takes to succeed. By extension, Ben is fully invested in sharing that knowledge with others.

I think of him as my brother because both of us want to help people like you be the best versions of yourselves. We're willing to lay everything on the line to help you achieve that goal.

Uncommon Leadership uncovers valuable lessons that will help you, no matter who you are or what challenges you face in your life. You will read about people who have carved out their distinct path with single-minded purpose, tenacity, ferocity, commitment, enthusiasm, energy, and fervor. What they share in common is that they are *all* uncommon! By this, I mean that there is no single path to success these people have taken to achieve their goals. They have blazed personal trails to arrive at an apex in life. Each also remains a work in progress, driven by an internal mechanism to keep reinvesting in themselves and elevating to an even higher state of being.

All of the people you will read about in *Uncommon Leadership* have refined their skills, discipline, and approaches and turned them into superpowers. They have developed those superpowers to such a high degree that they have earned the right to be called uncommon.

As you already know, people seek out uncommon, high achievers. By default, these achievers become role models and leaders by continuously and consciously activating their superpowers.

What are these superpowers? One of Coach Nick Saban's superpowers is that he works to a simple, single standard where process permeates every part of his coaching existence.

David Goggins's superpower is an uncommon mindset. He has weaponized his brain to reach rare mental plateaus and become the most physically fit man on the planet.

Four-time Olympian Chaunté Lowe beat a brutal form of breast cancer, using her superpowers to embrace and battle adversity instead of running from it.

Uncommon Leadership is also essential because Ben teaches that every one of us has our own superpowers: the one or two things that make each of us distinctive in others' lives. You may not ever take home the UFC Welterweight Championship belt like Tyron Woodley or win seven national championships like Coach Chris Klieman at North Dakota State University. But you can develop your superpowers into an uncommon standard and lead others to better lives as well.

Your superpowers are what God has gifted to you. Those superpowers can be a wicked sense of humor, the patience of a saint, a high musical IQ, the ability to heal others in mind and body, or natural athletic ability, to name a few. In *Uncommon Leadership*, Ben gives you the tools you need to more deeply explore your fullest potential so you can develop your own brand of uncommon leadership.

I often say you must be willing to do what others will not to lead a life that others can only dream about. As long as you're willing to do the work, you will discover your superpowers. When you do, you'll become an uncommon leader in your own life and the lives of others.

Uncommon Leadership provides you with pathways to unlock your potential and unleash your uncommon abilities.

INTRODUCTION

What is it that drives some men and women to rise above all others? How do they come to lead extraordinary lives? Is there a mindset or a belief system they have cultivated? And how is it that they inspire others through their thoughts, rituals, courage, and determination? What is it that drives these people to places of uncommon leadership?

I wanted to explore these ideas and seek answers by looking into the lives of some of the highest achievers I know and admire. I challenged myself to look beyond what the public knows about people like Jerry Rice, Coach Nick Saban, Jon Gordon, and other well-known figures. *Un-*

common Leadership is a chronicle of those efforts.

I will tell YOU this: there is never a single answer. Courage does not exist in a vacuum. Unshakable determination is a foundation that blends with unshakable purpose. And, as I've referenced many times in my other works like our podcast *The Burn*, committing to standards over feelings is an ongoing process that must combine other tools that work best for YOU. Not allowing YOUR feelings to dictate how YOU show up. But choosing to live to YOUR STANDARD to win each day. YOU must find a daily process that works for YOU. That process leads to what I call Your Prizefighter Day.

Process removes uncertainty. It allows leaders to create standards that become a code by which they live their lives. Much like prizefighters, those who adopt a superior mental edge that helps them to gain advantages win round after round and fight after fight. While all of these people share some things in common, there is also a visceral, distinct part of their makeup and how they approach the world. That uniqueness sets them apart. It makes them uncommon.

David Goggins lives his life through his uncommon mindset. Andy Frisella is frank when he tells YOU that being honest with yourself is the biggest mental barrier YOU may face. Tyron

Woodley keeps a tight circle of trusted friends, knowing that small circles can do big damage. And instead of running from adversity, Chaunté Lowe embraced the biggest challenge of her life and beat cancer with the same fervor she used to become a four-time Olympian.

Each of them has become an uncommon leader in the eyes of others by being true to themselves. Their single-minded purpose sets them apart from the vast majority of people in this world. Are they wired differently? Perhaps. Were they born that way? Probably not. This means that how they changed, what they sacrificed, and the success they have enjoyed is not limited to them by some divine measure. This should hearten YOU.

It means a personal path to uncommon leadership is YOURS if YOU want it. YOU have a choice.

YOUR path will be different than the people in this book because YOU are also unique. And YOU are uncommon, whether YOU know it or not.

It's up to YOU to turn your thoughts inward. YOU must get in touch with what drives YOU to excel. YOU must find what it is that can inspire YOU to rise above your current state in life. My friends in *Uncommon Leadership* will pique YOUR curiosity. I hope they'll ignite YOU to start YOUR own journey of discovery. But it's up to YOU to do the work. It's up to YOU to chart YOUR own course.

YOU can have more happiness, more success, better relationships, more money, and improved health—if YOU want. Some of the answers YOU seek are on these pages, and some of the answers have always been inside of YOU.

Go do great things.

Ben

1.

COACH NICK SABAN

THE WAY YOU DO ONE THING IS THE WAY YOU DO EVERYTHING

C oach Nick Saban is the most successful and well-known college football coach in America. He has won over 80 percent of the more than 300 college games he's coached at Toledo, Michigan State, LSU, and Alabama. Through the 2019 season, Coach Saban's teams had also won six NCAA National Championships. But his seventh national championship during the 2020 season has to rank as the most impressive accomplishments during his distinguished career. With a litany of challenges stacked against him and his program, many are even calling it the greatest team performance in college football history.

Although the COVID-19 pandemic impacted every facet of college football, including the Alabama program, Coach Saban and his team completely overwhelmed their opponents. That, despite the fact that he contracted the virus mid-season and was forced to quarantine until being cleared to return to the sidelines. Coach Saban seamlessly integrated three Heisman Trophy finalists (Mac Jones, Najee Harris, and winner DeVonta Smith) as the team steamrolled its way to a 13–0 record, including pummeling Ohio State in the National Championship game, 52–24.

With his seventh national championship victory, Coach Saban passed the legendary Paul "Bear" Bryant for the most national championship wins of all time, cementing his legacy as the greatest college football coach of all time. The only other time his Alabama team went undefeated was in 2009 when the Crimson Tide racked up a perfect 14–0 record. Seven other times in Coach Saban's career, his teams have lost only once in an entire season.

It's a waste of time even to discuss whether Coach Saban is a leader or not—he is. Much has already been written about Coach Saban's leadership skills. It would be an impossible task to delve into all of them. So instead, let's focus on what I consider to be one of the core philosophies he has used to mold his teams into champions.

Take a moment to absorb the implications of the following:

The way you do one thing is the way you do everything.

Break it down even further.

The way you do one thing . . .

. . . is the way you do everything.

Now pause for a moment. Let it sink in.

Do you want to be successful? Do you want to be a leader? If so, you, and only you, can hold yourself accountable for doing everything only one way. And only you know how deep you can dig to find and build a foundation of thought that becomes second nature, so that no matter what you do, you must approach *every* task the same way and with the same degree of high performance, self-accountability, and mental toughness, *every* time.

That's why, believe it or not, Coach Saban does not focus on results. Instead, he believes results are a direct product of process. Coach Saban didn't invent "the process," but there's a good chance he perfected it. The concept of "the process" has been embraced by some of the world's most successful people. John Wooden, Richard Branson, and the highly creative and successful teams at Apple and Disney are all proponents of focused process.

When it comes to process, Coach Saban is relentless. If you play for or coach with Coach Saban, there is a focus on how you do every task, large and small. Focusing on the process becomes the standard by which you hold yourself accountable. And when your process is pristine, your results will be optimal. It sounds easy. But when you're dealing with a locker room full of athletes and staff, it's a challenge.

Maintaining a high level of focus requires maintaining a presence in the here and now. Part of the process requires setting aside thoughts of the past and the future. There is only one moment in time, and that time is now. You must lock into the concept that when your thoughts drift, your process suffers. And when your process suffers, your results suffer, too.

In this regard, there can be no compromise. Every person connected with the Alabama program must fully commit to a process that requires intense present-moment focus. Everyone in the program must buy into this standard Coach Saban creates. You might know it better as team chemistry: every person on the same page, thinking the same way, with a common goal. Anything less has no place.

Also, consider this: mediocre people don't like high achievers, and high achievers don't like mediocre people. That means every player and coach must use every opportunity to improve individually so that the program can improve collectively.

The way you do one thing is the way you do everything.

Every player, which can loosely be defined as "the one thing," must perform to the best of their abilities so that the entire program, or "the everything," functions at peak performance. When that happens, you will get the best possible results.

Every choice matters. Every decision matters. And they either contribute to the goal of winning a championship, or they don't.

Is it easy? No.

Is it worthwhile? Only you can make that determination.

But when you choose "the process," the load becomes much lighter instead of heavier. You lose any thoughts of being selfish, you gain respect for your fellow teammates, and you eliminate useless clutter that can sidetrack your thoughts. When you buy into a collective philosophy that embraces focusing on the here and now, on the optimal performance of your task related to the overall goal, you engage in a disciplined approach that removes wasted thoughts and wasted actions. And when you follow Coach Saban's teachings, you also follow a process that has been time-tested for 25 years on one of the biggest and most competitive stages in America.

Still, you do have a choice. Nobody can make you buy into a philosophy or a process, although you would be wise to do so. Because, as Coach Saban explains it, "There are two pains in life. There is the pain of discipline and the pain of disappointment. If you can handle the pain of discipline, then you'll never have to deal with the pain of disappointment." When you focus on the way you do one thing and repeat that with focus over and over again, your process becomes how you do everything.

You can't be Nick Saban. But with focus and intensity, you can think like Nick Saban. And if you do, you will become an effective leader . . . guaranteed.

BEN'S TAKE

Working with the Alabama football program means you must be on your toes at all times. I remember my first one-on-one meeting with Coach Saban in his office. I don't recall all the specifics. I just remember walking out of that office and thinking to myself, "I've never seen an individual with that level of focus in my entire life." His meticulous attention to detail was like nothing I had ever experienced. You could immediately sense his level of commitment and the importance that he placed on his work. It was also readily apparent that he placed those same expectations on his players.

You can't always guarantee results, but you can always guarantee your process. Aim high, and even if you fall short of the big goal, your accomplishments will still be impressive. And those accomplishments will give you a higher starting point for what comes next.

To this day, when I walk into the Mal M. Moore Athletic Facility on the University of Alabama campus in Tuscaloosa, I always have to take a deep breath and recommit to Coach Saban's way of thinking. It is an unspoken moment of reflection that focuses on Coach Saban's sense of the here and now and his high-performance expectations for everyone associated with the program, including me. I am always grateful for that opportunity.

If there is anything uncommon about Coach Saban's ability to lead, it could be the simple beauty of his philosophy. Rather than muddy the waters with a long laundry list, Coach Saban's motivational efforts are brief and direct. Coach Saban and I share a passion for the process. This is the core of what I call the Prizefighter Day. A Prizefighter Day mentality is the framework that uses this passion for creating daily behaviors that lead to victories for those who buy into the philosophy. Coach Saban constantly creates prizefighter habits for his players. These prizefighter habits, stacked on top of each other, create Prizefighter Days. Prizefighter Days lead to wins on Saturdays. And prizefighter wins lead to prizefighter seasons.

If you walk on the sidelines for an Alabama practice as I often do, you'll hear echoes of "the way you do one thing is the way you do everything" laced throughout the session. It's reinforced by Coach Saban's corollary: "We do things right until we can't do them wrong." That is process talking—the ultimate attention to detail. That is how you win games and championships. It is how your team can step on to the field at Bryant-Denny Stadium in front of 101,821 fans with supreme confidence and with a plan that you have worked at, down to the smallest detail.

I have always believed in the "iron sharpens iron" mentality. Taken from the Old Testament scripture found in Proverbs 27:17, it more fully states, "As iron sharpens iron, so one man sharpens another." You must always stay sharp. For this to happen, strong and positive relationships are a necessity. It requires building a community of like-minded individuals who genuinely care about you and the collective outcome. That can only be the case when the person in charge holds themselves to this account.

Whether it is intentional or merely a by-product of how he leads others, Coach Saban stresses the collective by focusing on the individual. One man sharpens another man's efforts and performance through expectations based on an equality of mindset. Iron sharpens iron. And that applies whether you are a player, a coach, or a contributing motivator like me, grateful for the opportunity to work with a person who challenges me to get better every day.

I remain honored and humbled going forward as a performance coach for Coach Saban and his program. Without a doubt, the opportunity to play a part in the Alabama football team's success against the pandemic-related challenges of the 2020 season will stay with me forever.

YOUR PRIZEFIGHTER DAY

3 STEPS TO WIN THE DAY

STEP 1 - PERSONAL ACTIVITY

Example: Wake up every morning and get in some physical activity. It could be working out, walking, yoga, etc... We want to start the day feeling strong and confident. Get the endorphins flowing!

STEP 2 - BUSINESS ACTIVITY

Example: In a sales career, setting a specific goal for the number of phone calls or emails that you need to make (regardless of the result) that will grow your business.

STEP 3 - SERVICE ACTIVITY

Example: Reaching out to someone that is close to you and having a courageous conversation with them. Give back or lend your ears to a friend. No agenda, just service.

2.

JON GORDON

LEADING FROM THE HEART

You can't fake leading from the heart. Sooner or later, the people you're attempting to lead will figure it out. They'll know if you're deeply committed to your goals and to them, or if you're just biding time and going through the motions.

Jon Gordon committed to leading from the heart long ago. And now, it is one of the foundational philosophies that form his core belief system. It resonates, so when Jon dispenses advice, people listen.

As one of America's best-known experts on the subject of motivation, leadership, and building a positive workplace culture, Jon has authored more than 20 books. He has been a highly sought-after speaker by Fortune 500 companies, college and pro sports teams, schools, and others for years. Among his many insights, Jon will teach you that leading from the heart is all about leading with passion. When you find your source of passion and what inspires you, the challenge of leading others is much easier. Much like drawing water from a well, when you know what you value, what your goals are, and how you want to lead, the water level in the well is much higher. Dropping the bucket in and pulling out a full pail is a lot easier. Chances are, the water also tastes much sweeter.

If you know anything about Jon Gordon, you know the singular source of his passion is his Christian faith. It is the seed that gives birth to every other leaf on the tree of knowledge and wisdom he grows every day. How he ties in his faith and the concepts of leadership together is simple and straightforward. Jon's passion for spreading faith-based lessons of leadership is rooted in his conviction that Jesus is the greatest leader of all time. From there, the next step is easy to take: to be the best, you should learn from the best.

It blends with another part of Jon's narrative. He is also fully aware that to be a great leader, you must also be a great communicator. You must tailor your messages to your audiences so that they are easily understood and accepted. They won't listen to you, and you can't lead them if they've built walls and their guard is up. Recognizing that some people may be resistant to overtly Christian references, Jon has opted for a universal approach. That's why he couches biblical principles in secular language. Instead of trying to jump over preconceived walls about Jesus and Christianity, Jon walks through doors and delivers messages about leadership. He helps people become leaders and build great teams in places where a pastor probably wouldn't have the same impact.

Like all great leaders, Jon understands what motivates people and how human nature works, so he remains flexible, adjusting to changing conditions. There is no way you can do this unless you have passion. And that allows you to lead from the heart. It's impossible to work your hardest if you don't care as much as possible. There is no substitute for passion; there is only something less. You must be genuine in your efforts if you want to produce superior results.

Jon also understands that creating a dynamic and positive culture starts at the top. If you want your entire work culture to change, as a leader, it must begin with you. But even if you aren't the CEO, you can be a leader for whatever part of the organization you're responsible for.

Jon will tell you leadership is a transferred belief that combines passion and energy to transform the people around you. When you can articulate your organization's goals, values, and beliefs, by default, you become a leader, whether you're in the corner office or in the basement mailroom. It doesn't matter if you're responsible for 1,000 people or only yourself. A "leading from the heart" mindset is contagious. It will steel you and those around you against setbacks, rejections, and adversity when they happen. And those things will happen—guaranteed. So why wouldn't you do everything in your power to be as prepared as possible?

Leading from the heart produces positive energy. Jon detailed this idea in his book, *The Energy Bus: 10 Rules to Fuel Your Life, Work, and Team with Positive Energy*: "Positive energy is like a muscle. The more you use it, the stronger it gets. The stronger it gets, the more powerful you become. Repetition is the key, and the more you focus on positive energy, the more it becomes your natural state."

The other thing to remember is that while you may be a leader, you must always remember that people choose to let you lead them. They are always free to walk away—always. The higher you get in an organization, the more you must serve the people below you instead of having them serve you. You must serve their growth, their future, their careers, and their spirits, so they enjoy work and their lives. As a leader, the more you serve them, the more willing they will be to let you lead them.

And there is only one way you can achieve that. By leading from the heart.

BEN'S TAKE

Mentors need mentors. That's because truly wise men never stop learning. In my case, I am still learning from one of the best: my friend, my teacher, and my mentor—Jon Gordon.

Mentors challenge you. They provoke you to think in new ways. They freely give their time to you. They challenge your ways of thinking. And many times, they lead you to new levels of self-enlightenment.

Since I met Jon in 2008, he has done all of those things, over and over, again. However, the great gift Jon has bestowed upon me is the gift of faith. We met at a conference in San Antonio, where we were both speaking. Jon and I connected immediately. A week later, he called me to follow up. Although we had only spent about 20 minutes in our entire lives together, Jon questioned me about my faith during that call. He knew I had been raised Jewish, just like him, and that I had lost my mother at an early age.

He shared his faith journey with me and then ended our call with a challenge. Jon asked me to repeat the following prayer for 30 days, just to see what would happen:

God, what is my use for your purpose? Guide me towards that purpose. Jesus, if you are who you say you are, show me the signs. I'm open to receiving this if it's meant to be.

If you think it's uncommon for someone to be so bold as to ask you to do something like this right after first meeting them, you'd be right. If it happened to you, some of you might be turned off, rejecting the challenge out of hand. However, as I eventually figured out, it was simply Jon leading from the heart. I accepted the challenge, and I repeated it every day as Jon had requested.

I can't explain what happened next except to say that the impact was so profound that I accepted Christ before those 30 days were over. Maybe I was at a point in my life where I was ready for change. Perhaps it was divine intervention. All I know is that one small exchange with a man I had only just met continues to have an incredible impact on how I live my life to this day.

The act of accepting Christ, more than any other, challenges how I think. It challenges me in how I speak, in how I write. And it challenges me in how I can find passion and use it to motivate others to be the best possible version of themselves.

As a mentor, Jon has also helped me realize that we are never finished products as human beings. We are continually growing and changing. Every time I feel like I've grown into the person I should be, Jon is there as a reminder that I must continue to grow and change to become a better version of myself and what I am capable of achieving. Jon is the ground-zero source that tells me my work and growth are never done. In turn, I honor that insight by sharing with others that the growth and work are never done in all of us. If you know me, then this will have a familiar ring to it.

Jon is incredibly humble and reluctant to take any credit for his impact on my life. But I owe him a lot. I simply don't know how far my career would have gotten if not for his help. He told me the truth when I needed to hear it. He pushed me when I needed pushing. He gave me the example I needed to rise to the next level, many times over.

I'm telling you all of this for a reason: mentors need mentors. It's possible to be both a student and a mentor. Remember that. Because in your life, you *will* be both more often than not. Like Jon, you will have the opportunity to lead from the heart. You will also have the opportunity to follow from the heart. If you listen to what's inside of you, you will lead a good life, and you will lead others to their good lives, too.

"GOD, WHAT IS MY USE FOR YOUR PURPOSE? GUIDE ME TOWARDS THAT PURPOSE. JESUS, IF YOU ARE WHO YOU SAY YOU ARE, SHOW ME THE SIGNS. I'M OPEN TO RECEIVING THIS IF IT'S MEANT TO BE."

3.

WILL COMPTON

WINNING AS AN UNDERDOG BY USING A STANDARD OVER FEELINGS

As a two-way player on the North County High School football team in Bonne Terre, Missouri, Will Compton was anything but an underdog. In his senior year, he had 107 tackles, racked up 1,000 all-purpose yards, and scored 14 touchdowns. He was named first-team All-State by the Missouri Sportswriters and Broadcasters Association and followed that up by playing for the University of Nebraska.

As a Cornhusker, Will appeared in 50 games, including starting 37 games as a linebacker. He finished with 247 tackles, including 110 tackles in his senior year, and ranks 12th all-time in Nebraska's history. He was named a two-time All–Big 10 selection and a three-time Academic All–Big Ten selection along the way.

"Hardly the accomplishments of an underdog," you might say. And up until that point, you'd be right. However, Will's achievements are very much a part of his underdog story.

That's because, despite his stats and his hard-nosed play, he was told he was too slow and small to play in the NFL. He didn't receive an NFL Combine invitation. No NFL team drafted him after coming out of Nebraska.

Talk about a deflating experience, especially after Will enjoyed so much success up to that point in his career. With those kinds of setbacks, some players hang up their cleats, but not Will. Instead, he used them as motivation, as jet fuel for his competitive desires. The only difference was that for the first time in his life, Will was an underdog.

Will redoubled his efforts. He created goals that became the performance standard he set for himself. He silenced his negative emotions and refused to let those feelings become a barrier to his future success. Not easy things to do in a game that must be played with intensity and passion.

Framing your goals the right way at the right time is critical if you want to succeed. You must know when to set a standard for yourself and not let your feelings and emotions become barriers to that success. But even with the right mindset, your path is not necessarily easy or guaranteed. You must continue to believe in what you're doing, especially on the days when you don't feel like it. You must set a standard for yourself and block out those things that will mentally drag you down. Your daily process must not waver—no matter what challenges or setbacks you face. The right kind of hard work will pay dividends, as it eventually did for Will.

In 2013, the Washington Redskins signed him as an undrafted free agent. He started at the bottom of the NFL totem pole, ending up on the Redskins practice squad for the first 16 weeks of his rookie year. Will never quit trying to create a better version of himself. He kept working and wound up spending his first five seasons in the NFL with the Redskins. Instead of looking at an underdog mindset as an excuse for defeat, Will used those setbacks as a powerful motivational strategy.

In our own lives, whether our underdog status is true or not, when the perceived challenge is greater, all champions summon the next level of their competitive spirit. Winners can channel a "me against the world" mentality and transform it into a dynamic tool for success. You can lean on others for support. Ultimately though, you are responsible for how you think. When you take responsibility for your thoughts, you put yourself in charge of one of the few things you can control. In this way, you can develop your own standard for the challenges you face. It's not easy, but when you learn to set aside your feelings, you toss aside useless baggage, enabling you to focus on the thoughts and actions that matter.

The right way to adopt an underdog mindset is as a competitive advantage. As an underdog, many people expect little from you. But it's what you expect from yourself that counts. An underdog mindset brings focus and clarity of purpose when used as a challenge to overcome obstacles instead of as an excuse for defeat. The great thing is that when you persevere as an underdog, you become a role model for others to follow. People will gravitate to you as they follow your journey, many times because they want the same journey.

It does not happen by accident. Underdogs will experience defeats along the way. Refusing to let those setbacks get the best of you and turning them into springboards for success requires a lot of purposeful and directed thought. It means you must put aside the negative feelings of doubt, fear, and a lack of confidence. Instead, you must consciously continue to work towards the standard you have set for yourself, no matter what.

There's more to Will's story. If you have doubts about whether or not reframing the underdog mentality worked for him, consider that he went from being an undrafted free agent to being named a team captain for the 2016 season in three short years at Washington.

Underdogs often lead with their heart, but they also know they must summon an entire range of talents to put them on equal footing with their peers. Mental preparation and focus are more important when you're an underdog because there's less margin for error. As an underdog, creating a standard is not only how you survive—it's how you thrive. All that hard work will get you noticed. Change will occur. You will see results. These results may not be exactly what you had envisioned or come at the time and the place you want. Nobody can fully guarantee outcomes. Life is just that way.

You need to think in terms of measuring your success by teaching yourself how to think properly, recognizing this is a skill you can repeat over and over again for the rest of your life. Using all the tools you've been gifted with, including mental toughness, creates the right DNA for success.

Mental toughness gives you the ability to be both an underdog and successful in everything you do. If approached the right way, both can coexist inside of you.

You will encounter setbacks along your journey. If you don't, I will make the case that you aren't challenging yourself enough. Growth comes from setbacks even more than it comes from achievements. When you frame your setbacks into an underdog mentality and "draw a line in the sand" from which there is no retreat, you create a standard impervious to negative thoughts and feelings. You are leading yourself on the way through the journey that was meant for you. And in doing so, you will naturally lead others down a similar path as well.

BEN'S TAKE

Will Compton and I have been friends and brothers for a long time. It's a relationship born out of a common bond. We were both underdogs when we met back in 2013. Will had just signed with the Redskins as an undrafted free agent. I was in the process of selling my practice as a financial advisor and just starting to work full time at my coaching and speaking practice.

A mutual friend suggested that we connect because of the work I was doing with coaches and athletes. Will didn't know it at the time, but that consisted mainly of working with Ladue High School. By no coincidence at all, it's where I went to high school and once played on the basketball team. You have to start somewhere! And now, a few years later, that's exactly what Will and I were both doing.

Although I started my coaching and speaking work in 2006, I hadn't done anything in sports until 2011. But between that time and when I first met with Will, I had created a curriculum that is now part of *Your Mental Toughness Playbook*. The catch is that the concepts had never been tested before by a professional athlete.

I vividly remember meeting with Will at a Saint Louis–area Panera Bread restaurant. As an underdog, you have to summon every tool at your disposal to level the playing field. That's what Will and I did that day. He wanted next-level mental toughness. I wanted to put my concepts and curriculum to the test in a real-world situation.

I laid out the concepts. Will absorbed them like a sponge. By the time we were done, Will had completely embraced what I had put forth. The toughest part was done, in some ways, because mentally, he had flipped a switch and bought in.

Napoleon Hill said it best, and you've probably heard it before: "What the mind can conceive and believe, it can achieve." An underdog's mental toughness is critical. That was the case for both of us in those days.

But it doesn't end there. You have to take that mental toughness and put it into action. Obviously, many elements go into becoming successful in your chosen field, whether it's coaching, playing professional sports, succeeding in business, or winning in any endeavor you choose. However, the thing that's common to all of these is starting from a place of mental toughness. You must set a standard for yourself and be unshakable and unwavering as you work toward your goals.

The bottom line is that Will Compton trusted me. He trusted that I could help him. The rest, as they say, is history. Will Compton went on to play eight years in the NFL. He went from being an undrafted free agent to team captain of the Redskins in three short seasons.

Using my own ideas about mental toughness, I've gone on to do pretty well in my own right, too. Will and I forged our relationship in a common bond shared by two underdogs. How much does that bond mean? I'll tell you one of my favorite stories that reveals the depth of our relationship. It's also one of the best examples of uncommon leadership and friendship I can ever hope to live through.

In his first NFL playoff game, Will played and started against Aaron Rodgers and the Green Bay Packers. I flew in right after watching North Dakota State, who I was working with as a performance coach, win a national football championship. Even though the Redskins came up short, I was so proud of Will's performance.

When I arrived at the team hotel the evening before, I walked into the hotel room. Will had left in my room the first-ever game ball that he had received. If you know anything about getting a game ball, you know what a big deal this is. Will gave the game ball to me. *He gave the game ball to me*—to me. To this day, it's still one of the greatest gifts I've ever been given. I'm going to keep it for a while. And at some point, I'm going to give it back, but probably not to Will. I'm going to give it to his children.

Then I'm going to tell them the story of how I got the ball and explain to them the kind of man their father is. The bond of the underdog is strong. And it's going to be with Will and me forever.

STANDARD

To truly be the best of the best, high achievers don't allow FEELINGS to dictate how they show up.

We all go through tough times in our lives, but the greatest of the great accept those setbacks. They embrace challenges as part of life. And if the purpose is significant enough, they continue to FIGHT with everything they have.

But many others show up and allow feelings to dictate their performance.

That's why the most SUCCESSFUL people in life live to a STANDARD and not their FEELINGS.

OVER
FEELINGS

4.

COACH CHRIS KLIEMAN

FIND YOUR EDGE IN THE DETAILS

During his coaching career, Chris Klieman has learned a thing or two about finding an edge and using it to his best advantage. Without a doubt, there are many talented and successful football coaches in America, but it's an elusive edge that sets elite coaches, winners, and leaders apart from others.

Competition is fierce. So, to find that edge, you must dig deeper than your opponent. You must drill down and comprehend that the minutia of your challenge can spell the difference between winning or not. When you do, that's where you'll find your edge: in the details.

For those not willing to put in the work, the devil is in the details. For Coach Klieman, the *edge* is in the details. The obvious question then becomes, "Which details?"

It's not an easy question to answer because your details will be different than everyone else's. But in all cases, uncovering crucial details requires conscious thought on your part. It requires building a mindset of deeply held beliefs and principles tested over time and putting them to work for you. Drilling down to the details doesn't only require thinking outside the box; it requires building a whole new box to store your thoughts and knowledge. That's what Coach Klieman has done.

Check this out: in a game where success is typically measured in wins and losses, Coach Klieman does not focus on wins and losses. Say what? How can that be?

That's because he focuses on the process instead. Ah! A most important detail. The irony is that by not focusing on wins and losses, he has produced one of the most enviable won-loss records in college football.

Consider: as a head coach at North Dakota State University, his teams won 92 percent of the time, including a perfect 15–0 season for his 2018 Bison team. That was only the fifth team in Football Championship Subdivision history to go undefeated on the way to a national championship. Overall, Coach Klieman guided the Bison to four national championships in five years as a head coach after helping lead them to another three national championships as the team's defensive coordinator. In the end, he was a part of seven of NDSU's national championships, the most in FCS history. Here's another remarkable stat. Chris Klieman coached teams that never lost two consecutive games . . . for 14 seasons!

With much of the pressure of winning and losing removed, players are free to focus on the process instead. They zero in on getting a little bit better every day. When they focus on their own details and all the collective details are added together, the team produces incredible results.

Taking a process-based approach means that players don't have to make any one moment bigger than it needs to be, which removes undue pressure on them to perform. Focusing on the future and the intended result often only makes things worse. But when players focus on one play at a time, their thoughts, reactions, and judgments are quicker and more accurate. The onus of having to go out and score on a drive, win a game, or become bowl-eligible can be a heavy burden to carry. On the other hand, focusing on the process in the here and now removes that burden.

Or, to put it in Coach Klieman–speak, he encourages players to "win every dang day." You attack Monday and win it to get to Tuesday. You attack Tuesday and win it to get to Wednesday. You don't attack Wednesday to win it and then jump straight to Saturday. Instead, the primary goal is to go 1–0 every day. When players stack up several 1–0 days, it dramatically improves the odds of going 1–0 on game days.

He also teaches his players to approach the season as 12 one-week seasons instead of one 12-week season. It's a seemingly small detail with a big ripple effect. The ancillary benefit of a here-and-now approach is that it focuses on tight-knit relationships between the players and coaches. That family-first philosophy builds a cohesive environment that gives Coach Klieman's teams a decided edge. His holistic approach to relationships preaches going all in for yourself, your teammates, and in everything you do.

That not only makes it possible to win today, it also sets you up to wake up to tomorrow with the best possible chance of winning that day as well. When you lay a strong foundation one day, you start at a naturally elevated position the next day and every day after that. That philosophy has impacted hundreds of players throughout Klieman's career. But no player relationship has been more high profile than that between Coach Klieman and Carson Wentz. That bond and Carson's story are worth telling because Carson's journey is also a teachable example of uncommon leadership.

Influenced by Coach Klieman, Carson learned how to lead with faith over fear by playing for an Audience of One.

Whatever you do, work at it with all your heart,
as working for the Lord, not for human masters.

This scripture in Colossians 3:23 is prominently displayed on Carson's charitable foundation website. It reveals a man who has channeled his faith and considerable athletic gifts for the good of people less fortunate than him. That belief in putting others first and in the family of humanity has roots in how Carson was raised. But it was also brought more sharply into focus and reinforced under Coach Klieman, who provided the framework Carson needed to realize his full potential.

Through his college accomplishments, as a successful NFL quarterback, and as a man of deeply convicted faith, Carson Wentz has become a leader on and off the field. In 2013, at the start of his freshman year at North Dakota State University, senior quarterback Dante Perez began mentoring Carson in his faith. Dante became a huge influence, igniting an even bigger passion for the Lord in Carson. Carson became an active member of the team Bible study, a regular church attendee, and routinely shared his testimony with people on campus.

It's also worth noting that while Carson played at NDSU under Coach Klieman's guidance, the team also won five national championships. Carson drew a lot of attention and exceeded all expectations when he was drafted second overall by the Philadelphia Eagles, making him the highest Division 1 AA pick ever.

Combining his faith, hard work, and an exceptional set of God-given skills, Carson justified that pick by leading the Eagles to an 11–2 record in his second year, before going down with an ACL injury. At the time, he had already broken several Eagles and NFL records and tossed 33 touchdown passes, the second highest in the league. Even though his season ended early, he coached from the sidelines, and his leadership was an integral part of the Eagles winning the Super Bowl that year.

Carson has combined his faith and initial success in the NFL and founded the AO1 Foundation in 2017. AO1 is short for "Audience of One," a reference to Jesus and a direct reflection of Carson's faith. Many people are successful in all walks of life. But those who find motivation and inspiration and are openly willing to share the source of their strength are the ones who become leaders.

The AO1 Foundation melds Carson's upbringing, those who have influenced him, and his religious beliefs. The foundation focuses on serving underprivileged youth, the physically disabled, and military veterans, all "to demonstrate the love of God." These groups enjoy nature and wildlife activities that reflect some of Carson's most cherished passions in life: his faith, his enthusiasm for the outdoors, and his avid love for dogs.

In the same way he approaches everything else in life, Carson has racked up several "wins" since forming the AO1 Foundation. He funded and built a sports complex in Haiti and formed Thy Kingdom Crumb to feed and distribute food in at-risk communities. His Outdoor Ministry serves people with physical challenges and life-threatening illnesses through hunting and fishing outings and through his Camp Conquerors program.

Carson has proven, time and again, that leaders don't just lead; they do the tough work—in the trenches, where it counts. But true leaders understand you must find motivation and inspiration that strengthen your resolve. When your willpower is unbreakable, it allows you to overcome any fears of failure. Faith and inspiration provide focus and clarity that will lead you to the goals in your life.

In Carson's case, the choice of faith over fear is not only his personal success story. Part of the story also belongs to Coach Klieman for helping mold Carson into the man he is today. The result is that Carson's life has evolved into choosing to make the world a better place through an unshakable and deep-seated belief in an Audience of One. And has given us a lesson in uncommon leadership from which we can all learn.

Coach Klieman's repeatable approach to leadership has continued to pay dividends for his current team, Kansas State. In his 2019 inaugural season, after being picked to finish ninth in the Big 12 Conference, Coach Klieman's team racked up eight wins, finishing third. Those eight wins were the most in school history for a first-year coach and included an eye-opening win against No. 5 Oklahoma at home: the first such win since 1996. Those results didn't go unnoticed. A little more than one season into his Wildcats tenure, he received a generous multi-year extension to his contract that runs through the 2026 season.

Coach Klieman's impact has also produced a ripple effect that extends beyond the playing field. In a single season at Kansas State, his Wildcats placed a school-record 32 players on Academic All-Big 12 teams, including a league-record 26 first-team members.

That's just one example among many of his off-field accomplishments. There is another essential detail that Coach Klieman brings to his life's work: you must love what you do.

Read it again: you must *love* what you do. It's not enough to "really like" your job. You can't lead others if you can't demonstrate a passion for your work. You must love what you do in order to give you the edge you need to be a strong and effective leader.

Focus on process . . . Focus on family . . . Focus on the here and now . . . Focus on loving what you do. And you will also win—"every dang day."

BEN'S TAKE

I'm not lying when I tell you I was a bit baffled when Coach Klieman first asked me to come and speak to his players. For a team that has won four straight FCS national championships, there's only so much you can say or do to build upon the success they had already achieved at NDSU. You have to take an uncommon approach to leadership when you're coming into a program that appears to be at the top of its game.

As I began to dig a little deeper into the coach and his program, it dawned on me that Coach Klieman was not about living in the glories of the past. He was more concerned about replicating successful processes and doing the hard work to keep his team performing at the highest possible level for the season ahead. That's when I realized his desire to keep getting better, coupled with finding ways to motivate young men on the field every game, actually made my job easier. I was there to keep stoking the fire, help the program maintain focus, and build on a foundation that had already achieved so much.

Coach Klieman's mindset, attention to detail, and personal commitment to every person in the program made it easy for him to motivate me to buy into the NDSU culture. I think this mindset is also why Coach Klieman and Carson Wentz formed such a close bond with each other.

As a leader, Coach Klieman was actually serving his team by doing everything he could to create an optimal winning environment. When I met Carson Wentz, I soon discovered that he also believed that to be an effective leader, you must also learn to be a good servant.

You may have come across this connection between leadership and servanthood before. It's not new or unique, although if you're not aware, it will strike you as an uncommon way to approach leadership. On the surface, these two propositions appear to be polar opposites. In reality, they're not. They are closely joined at the hip, like two brothers—like Coach Klieman and Carson Wentz. And when they're practiced in concert with each other, they form a rock-solid foundation to build and grow your life and those you lead, whether it's on the field, in a board room, or at home with your family.

Coach Klieman and Carson know that one of the foundational keys to effective leadership is motivating your people. If you can't inspire others, the only other way to lead is by force. And who wants to lead others that way? Motivation is also a two-way street: two sides of the same leadership coin. To be the best leader possible, you have to be motivated by those you lead. You have to care.

If you ask your people to have skin in the game, then you must have skin in the same game as well. They'll spot your lack of commitment a mile away, and without reciprocal motivation, you'll never have the best possible outcome, no matter what you're doing. That's why nobody works harder than Coach Klieman and Carson Wentz.

Of course, you can't always control the outcome on the field, but you can control the amount of effort you put in to be ready to play your best game. Both men understand this, and it's one of the big keys to all they have accomplished. When a Chris Klieman–coached team or an offense led by Carson Wentz takes the field, it's only after they have given everything they have, leading up to game day. In this way, they lead by serving.

Through my work with Carson Wentz, Coach Klieman, and his players, I was blessed to be part of the national championship team at North Dakota State University during Carson's senior year. It was a record-breaking, fifth straight national championship, a record almost certain to never be broken. We all received championship rings signifying our accomplishment. People are always impressed when they see the ring. Many can't believe how big it is and how many diamonds there are in it.

But for me and many others who were a part of that experience, when we look at the ring, we see something completely different. I look at it, and I see relationships with all the players I came to know and respect, forged in the fight for a common goal.

Flashback to the first time I spoke to the team: they had just won their fourth straight national championship. Quite frankly, I had no idea what to say or why they were bringing me in to speak. And then it dawned on me: I was there to play a part in motivating them and leading them to another great season. I was there to serve them. Reframing my purpose created the answers I need to help this incredible group of young men.

Sitting in the front row was Carson Wentz, attentively setting the standard, as a leader should. I didn't know it at the time, but Carson, the Bisons' leader on the field, was already openly pursuing a higher cause at the time. He was serving Jesus off the field, simultaneously leading others to His teachings.

Leaders like Carson Wentz understand that the nature of relationships depends on give and take. For a relationship to mean anything, whether it's football, spiritual matters, or anything else in life, you must be a leader *and* a servant. Carson continues to serve and lead, on the playing field on Sundays and off the field as well, through ongoing work with his AO1 Foundation.

So does Coach Klieman. On the outside, many people only see national championships and NCAA records. From the inside, because I am perpetually a student of the best practices on motivating and leading others, I can assure you that Coach Klieman is not only one of the greatest coaches of athletic teams; he is also one of the most extraordinary human beings I have ever met.

He doesn't simply build winning football teams; he builds winning individuals, on and off the field. This is his edge, his competitive advantage. And this is why he has been able to take that philosophy and duplicate it at Kansas State. He understands what is universal and can translate it into what is personal for the players he coaches.

That has continued to make my job much easier, too. The concept of culture is slightly different at Kansas State than at NDSU, but the principles are the same. At Kansas State, Coach

Klieman's edge is teaching players to "win every dang day." My job is to reinforce that mantra.

In fact, that's how "Pound the Stone," a concept derived from my friend Joshua Medcalf's best-selling book by the same title, was born. "To drive home the philosophy, I introduced a sledgehammer as the unofficial team mascot for the Wildcats. It's a symbolic reminder that to stay on top of your game at all times, you must show up every day. You must be relentless; you must pound the stone.

That's because showing up every day and doing your best is a choice. Deciding to give it everything you've got—every damn day—is a choice.

Coach Klieman knows this. His players know it. And now, so do you.

WIN THE DANG DAY

Taking a process-based approach means YOU don't have to make any one moment bigger than it needs to be, removing undue pressure on YOU to perform.

POUND THE STONE

5.

DREW HANLEN

REVERSE ENGINEER YOUR SUCCESS IN THE
UNSEEN HOURS

Drew Hanlen is one of the most sought-after basketball skills trainers in the world today. His roster of players includes NBA stars Joel Embiid, Bradley Beal, Jayson Tatum, Zach LaVine, and hundreds of other high-level competitors. He has consistently delivered results by building on the foundational philosophy that success comes from the work you put in during the "unseen hours."

The "unseen hours" are precisely what they sound like: it's the work you put in when nobody else is watching. It's the inner drive required to stay focused and to practice with purpose for as many hours as it takes to master the task in front of you. The key to maximizing your unseen hours is to reverse engineer your way to your desired outcome.

Here's what that means. By way of example, it's not enough to generally know how to shoot a three-pointer from beyond the arc. To succeed, you need to break down every individual element of that process that will lead you to make the shot with the highest possible frequency; this is the "reverse engineering" part. With a three-pointer, as it is with any task in life, to be successful, not only must you break down the parts of the shot into the smallest of elements, you must also master each of those elements. You must square your shoulders to the basket, elevate quickly, rise above the defender, make sure your hands are placed correctly on the ball, release at the height of your jump, put the right rotation and arc on the ball, and follow through with a smooth and fluid shooting motion. You must be willing to understand each of these individual components' intricacies and nuances, then practice and refine them until each piece fits perfectly as part of an overall motion designed to produce a positive outcome.

To succeed, you must practice each of these components for as long as it takes to master each one. It's not something you can do during a game. By that time, you've either mastered the skill, or you haven't. The hard work of perfecting the shot takes place in the unseen hours.

When you step on the court, if you've done the work, you'll do so with confidence, and you'll give yourself every opportunity to help your team win. Conversely, if you haven't done the work, your coach will know, your teammates will know, the fans will know, opposing players will know, and worst of all, you'll know it, too. I guarantee you, that's not a good feeling to have.

There's no denying that natural talent will give you an advantage in anything you undertake. But if you're not the most naturally talented player on the court or in life, you can balance the scales by outworking everyone else. Tenacity as a mindset is the great equalizer in life.

This is part of what Drew teaches as well. And it's backed by his own real-life experiences. He wasn't always the most physically gifted player on the court, but he discovered early on that he had the mental toughness it took to be a winner. As a player on the Webster Groves (Missouri) High School basketball team, Drew would get up every morning and shoot 1,000 shots before classes, missing only four days of that routine in four years. He played a key role in helping Webster Groves and his college team, Belmont University (Tennessee), to their best all-time winning seasons in each program's history. His tenacity in the unseen hours transformed 1,000 daily shots into results on the court. He shot nearly 50 percent from beyond the three-point line as a senior at Belmont. In fact, he finished the 2011–12 season ranked second in all of NCAA Division I, nailing an eye-popping 48.2 percent of his three-point shots.

When you put in the kind of work and produce the type of results Drew has, people will notice. Like Drew, when you put in the work in the Unseen Hours, people with drive and ambition will seek you out, learn from you, or partner with you. Your peers will consult with you and seek advice because they know that you know what it takes to succeed. They are well aware that your success did not happen by accident. And this is how you will become a leader.

As a leader, you must continue to demonstrate a commitment to your process. You must continue to put in your work in the unseen hours. Only when you set the bar high for yourself can you set it high for others. When you mentally, physically, and emotionally accept that you can reverse engineer your way to success in the unseen hours, you will become a leader through your actions and achievements.

BEN'S TAKE

When you count the top motivational experts in the world among your friends, you can expect that you'll often mix business with pleasure. Some might call it an occupational hazard, but if you're fully wired into being the best possible version of yourself and you're committed to making others the best possible version of themselves, then an "occupational hazard" is actually an "occupational opportunity."

That's what it's like to spend time with Drew Hanlen. There is no "off" switch; I get treated the same way he treats his NBA player clients. Honestly, I wouldn't want it any other way. It energizes me the same way Drew energizes a power forward to work on his low post game or a shooting guard to add percentage points to his made three-point attempts.

Drew and I often push each other. We seamlessly move from mentor to mentee and back again. He wouldn't be a true friend if he let me settle for less. The same applies in holding him accountable to a high standard.

You have people in your life like this. Those in your inner circle are probably there because they bring value to your life. They challenge you and encourage you to excel; they give you legitimate feedback, good and bad. Your inner circle will tell you the truth, even when you may not want to hear it. That inner circle dialog is the only way you can dissect and reverse engineer your life obstacles.

Breaking things down into their smallest pieces often reveals solutions that you can't always see when trying to see the whole of the situation. When you can listen, analyze, change course, and solve problems, you will become a leader. Problem solvers are leaders, and those who find creative ways to achieve desired outcomes are uncommon leaders.

Reverse engineering your way to a solution and then putting in the unseen hours to implement that solution won't happen unless you are ready to commit fully to that process. Drew Hanlen strongly believes that if you can't get your mind right, then no amount of coaching will change your outcomes in a meaningful way. A desire for the best possible outcome starts from within, and nobody but you can make that commitment.

One of the ways Drew and I do this is to create "I Am" statements; these are short declarations that help you visualize where you want to go. They help you see the person you believe you can be.

I go into greater detail about developing effective "I Am" statements in *YOUR Mental Toughness Playbook*. For now, you simply need to understand that "I Am" statements provide you with an internal and focused challenge. Here are some examples:

- "I am going to buy my own home before I'm 30."
- "I am going to lose 40 pounds over the next four months."
- "I am going to get my MBA and advance my career within the next three years."

You have to be ready to close the gap between the person you are and the person you want to be. That is where Drew and I both start our journeys when we work with someone in the beginning.

Desire is the foundation of passion; passion is the foundation of mental toughness. Mental toughness is the foundation for developing a standard for yourself and the right standard, intelligently and diligently applied, creates success.

When you work through this sequence, you

might be surprised to find out you're a lot closer than you think to achieving your goals. Optimizing your life this way can lead you to more happiness, more confidence, a better job, a nicer home, or whatever it is that your desires are.

And that includes becoming an uncommon leader.

I AM

YOUR "I AM" Statements are the answers to the "Who are YOU??" question. You have the ability to answer this question based upon the person that you are or based upon the person you believe you have the talents to become. Either way, YOUR "I AM" Statements will drive your beliefs toward thinking bigger for yourself.

Remember the key is challenging yourself to think bigger than the person that you currently are and the things that you have already achieved. Connect to the person you desire becoming and grab your future and bring it to today.

Take the example of Muhammad Ali. Ali had the unbelievable confidence in himself in believing, "I AM the heavyweight champion of the world" before he achieved that goal. Nobody else thought it was possible, but Muhammad Ali believed and he surrounded himself with advocates who believed in him, supported him, loved on him and inspired him grow. For Ali this was more productive than surrounding himself with adversaries who believed against him.

When you look at the story of Muhammad Ali, not only did he become the heavyweight champion of the world, but he is now recognized as one of the greatest athletes to ever walk this earth.

What do you believe YOU are capable of achieving?? What are YOUR "I AM" Statements?

6.

ANDY FRISELLA

LEADERSHIP IS NOT FOR EVERYBODY

Why would you pull together a book on uncommon leadership and then risk turning off some of your readers by highlighting a man who says leadership is not for everybody? This is why: because you're telling Andy Frisella's story.

Leadership, uncommon or otherwise, is not easy. It requires honesty, accepting reality, telling the truth to others as well as yourself, and setting your ego aside. Andy will tell you that some people can do this, and some people cannot. If this sounds daunting to you, that's because it is. But Andy will be the first to tell you he is no different than you; he has gone through the same kinds of adversity, doubts, fears, and trauma. That's why Andy Frisella knows you can become an uncommon leader and a master of your own life if you really want to. But Andy will also tell you that not everyone is willing to make that commitment.

Like most of us, Andy started from humble beginnings. He and his business partner didn't have fancy MBA degrees or wealthy benefactors. Andy was an admittedly poor student throughout school. He got into scuffles along the way, too. In fact, he still bears facial scars from a knife fight that almost cost him his life.

What Andy did have, however, was a father who believed in him. His dad, Big Jim, taught him the most valuable lesson of his entire life: the right mindset is everything, and that mindset is rooted in mental toughness.

Armed with this valuable kernel, in 1999, Andy Frisella and his high school buddy, Chris Klein, started Supplement Superstores while they were students at Southwest Missouri State University. Their initial seed money amounted to the $12,000 they had earned from painting stripes in parking lots. Andy and Chris made seven dollars on their first day in business, and that was only because a friend bought something because he felt sorry for them. Strapped for cash, they lived at the store, sleeping on mattresses in the back and showering at a local gym more often than not. It took eight full months for the store to break $200 in sales for a single day. For ten years, they boot-strapped it, slowly growing and refusing to quit.

If you've ever struggled, lived with doubt, or wondered if there has to be a better way, then you and Andy Frisella have a lot in common. But if you're still stuck in those places, this is where you and Andy Frisella are different.

Even after several years of scraping by, nothing had really clicked until they admitted their shortcomings. Adversity led to introspection: Andy and Chris were honest with themselves.

Introspection soon morphed into action. That's when they moved from a "sell a customer something at all costs" mentality and began to invest in relationships with everyone who walked in their door. It cemented what Andy likes to refer to as the "power of perspective."

Despite the adversity of those early years, Andy could put things into perspective by finding the good in the bad. He realized that there are things we can't control. There are times when frustration and anger will make you want to quit. Sooner or later, adversity visits everyone. Some people are not willing to endure those setbacks, not willing to make the necessary changes to become more successful. And some people do not have the capacity or willingness to embrace their adversity and become leaders of their own lives. In this way, leadership is not for everybody.

Here's the truth: you can't lead others until you first learn to lead yourself. Learning from your setbacks is only part of the key to success. Making changes is the other.

When Andy began focusing on relationships instead of sales, he went from making pocket change on his first day in business to where he's at today: nine figures in annual sales. He's launched several successful business ventures, including Supplement Superstores, 1st Phorm, Alpine Sports Products, Carbon Fire Nutrition, Paradise Distribution, 44Seven Media, and others.

You might also be surprised to know that Andy has also written a best-selling series of children's books that promote entrepreneurial values. How's that for a prime example of mental toughness removing self-limiting boundaries?

Andy now freely mentors and motivates others by sharing his story and keys to success. From 2015 to 2019, he hosted The MFCEO Project, the number-one business and success podcast in the world. Andy also created 75 Hard, a mental toughness program geared toward individual success, built on 20 years of real-life experiences. He co-founded the Arete Syndicate with Ed Mylett, an elite group of entrepreneurs focused on the synergy of scaling their businesses and reaching personal goals with terminal efficiency.

You may be reading this and feeling discouraged because it feels like you're so far away from your personal goals. You may think you don't have it in you to be an uncommon leader. You could even think that serendipity played a part in Andy's success. And yet, nothing could be further from the truth.

If Andy Frisella has only one thing to teach you about uncommon leadership, it is this: everything you need is already inside of you. Andy is a common man with an uncommon way of thinking. The good news is, there is not a limited supply of how much mental toughness is in this world. It's out there, and it's yours for the taking, but you have to want it. Otherwise, uncommon leadership is not for you.

BEN'S TAKE

One of the best, most indispensible qualities any leader can have is honesty. To be successful in a meaningful and sustainable way, you need to be honest with your customers, employees, family, and friends. But even beyond that, the kind of honesty I'm talking about is being honest with yourself.

This is where Andy Frisella excels. I have known him for some time, and as simple as that kind of honesty may sound, it was not always an easy thing for him to do.

To succeed, we have internal voices that prop us up, get us through the tough times, and feed our brains with messages that allow us to create mental toughness. But the downside of this is that sometimes, our ego gets in the way. We confuse our ego with reality, or the two openly compete for our attention, and that creates conflict. That happens to a lot of people. It's frustrating when you think you're doing everything you should to be successful, and you're still not.

We often don't realize that the missing piece is to be honest with ourselves: to recognize when something is not working. When we fail at this, our ego and our pride, usually necessary allies to drive us, fall out of alignment and actually become barriers to achieving bigger goals.

Andy's story is an object lesson in self-honesty. For ten years, he struggled. Eventually, Andy set aside his ego, pride, and his failures. He was honest with himself. Like all great men and women, he looked inward for the answers. He took the harsh reality of limited success and turned it into a lesson to be learned.

Then he used those lessons to make changes. He transformed his business model and his life by placing a priority on relationships. Andy recognized that we all want to be valued. We all want attention and validation that we matter.

Does it take time? Absolutely! Does it always pay off? Not always. Does it work?

Ask Andy—although you already know the answer.

People, by their very nature, are social animals. Genuine social interaction feeds a deep-seated need to belong. It is instinctual to want to be part of a community. Andy has built several highly successful businesses incorporating this concept and then taking necessary steps to solve his customers' problems. He freely shares this philosophy. Like Andy himself, this is a straightforward approach to life; there is no need to overly complicate this idea. Make people feel good, and they will want to be around you. Everyone wants a great customer experience, but Andy never would have gotten there if he didn't shift his way of thinking.

Andy inspires me through his example. By creating 75 Hard he gave me the opportunity to unlock more of my potential by tapping more of my mental toughness. That's right: as Coach Saban has taught us, iron sharpens iron. Just because we have our own Mental Toughness Academy doesn't mean I can't get better. We must all check our egos at the door, choose to improve, and continue to attack the obstacles to reaching our very best.

"Honesty is the best policy" may sound a little old-fashioned. You have to give Andy Frisella credit; he updated and reinvented that notion in an increasingly techno-disjointed world. What is old is new again, and sometimes what is simple, tried, and true is overlooked. Many times, in fact, simple is smart. The "human factor," when combined with internal honesty, roll-up-your-sleeves dedication, and hard work, will produce results.

Not everyone has the will to do this, and not everyone has the will to become a leader. Can you be honest with yourself? If so, you may be well on your way to becoming an uncommon leader, too.

7.

TYRON WOODLEY

SMALL CIRCLES CREATE BIG DAMAGE

A t first blush, it's an odd title for a chapter. In fact, you may be asking yourself how small circles and big damage tie into leadership. Here's how.

Typically, the goal of an organization is to build and grow. You do that by creating as many positive outcomes as possible to advance your mission. But if you are a mixed martial arts fighter like Tyron Woodley, your ability to create positive outcomes for yourself is directly linked to inflicting physical damage on your opponent in the octagon. The former UFC Welterweight Champ of the World and future UFC Hall of Famer has been highly successful on both counts.

Developing a warrior mentality and beating some of the best in the sport has not always been easy for someone perennially labeled as an underdog. But Tyron has always refused to listen to doubters and naysayers. Instead, he has repeatedly called upon a deep well of inner strength born from his faith. He has kept a small circle of friends, coaches, and family members close who believed in him. To this day, Tyron remains energized by both, giving him pinpoint focus in and out of the fight game.

Tyron understands you don't need a lot of people to support you, as long as you have the right people in your life to support you. His approach is decidedly uncommon in a world often consumed by "hits," "likes," and heart emojis. And that's how small circles can create big damage.

Tyron grew up in Ferguson, Missouri, the eleventh of thirteen children. After his father left, the family struggled, barely scraping by for many years. But while they lacked creature comforts, his mother, Deborah, would not let any of her children make excuses. She combined love, support, and compassion with a tough and tight-knit approach to her family that redirected Tyron away from drugs, gangs, and poverty.

He excelled as an athlete and a student in high school. Overcoming the odds and naysayers, Tyron was a mainstay on the McCluer High School honor roll while also becoming a Missouri state wrestling champion and a two-time high school All-American. During his senior year, he posted a perfect 48–0 record at 165 pounds. Even more impressive, Tyron didn't cede a single point on the mat unless he allowed an opponent to regain his feet. It was a perfect record of creating big damage and a preview of bigger things yet to come.

In his redshirt year at the University of Missouri, he racked up a 47–7 record, beating two of his three opponents who were ranked in the top 10 in the country in his weight class. Tyron became a Big XII wrestling champion and a two-time NCAA Division 1 All-American before eventually becoming a wrestling coach at his alma mater.

Upon entering the MMA world, he combined inspiration and perspiration to make a big splash in MMA, knocking out his first UFC opponent in just 36 seconds and winning his first seven bouts either by knockout or submission. Eventually, he became the welterweight champion by pummeling Robbie Lawler in just two minutes and 12 seconds, the fastest welterweight title fight finish in UFC history.

When asked who his heroes are, he'll tell you they are Jesus, his mom, and Muhammad Ali . . . in that order. Tyron draws strength from many sources, but he undoubtedly draws the most inspiration from his faith.

When he's in training, Tyron does MMA sparring and conditioning three days a week. He boxes, live wrestles, and runs three other days a week. On Sunday, the Lord's Day, he attends "Spiritual Bootcamp."

Other fighters choose intimidating ring nicknames, like Wanderlei "The Axe Murderer" Silva, Quinton "Rampage" Jackson, or Carlos "The Natural Born Killer" Condit. They do this to brand themselves and get inside the head of their opponents.

Not Tyron. His nickname is The Chosen One, a direct reference to Jesus—which, upon reflection, may be the most intimidating of all. Tyron is not afraid to lead with his faith.

He has parlayed his success in the octagon into many ventures, appearing in several television and film roles and as an analyst and commentator for the UFC. He has hosted a weekly segment on TMZ, curates a YouTube channel with two million views, and even collaborated with Wiz Khalifa and T-Dubb-O to release a music single.

But he has not forgotten where he has come from. Giving back to the young people in his community as the ATT Evolution MMA and Fitness gym owner in Brentwood, Missouri, is a priority for Tyron. He invests time with at-risk youth through his **PS** Protocol mentoring program, leading susceptible minds away from bad influences and giving them the greatest of all possible gifts instead: hope.

Tyron has become a leader by becoming a role model. Surrounded by a small group of people he trusts and driven by his faith in Jesus, he has used his success as a platform to change lives for the better.

Tyron *is* inflicting damage. But it's the right kind of damage: against despair, against a lack of self-confidence, and against other negative challenges so many people fight to overcome, every moment of every day.

Small circles *do* create big damage. And that's a lesson in leadership worth knowing.

BEN'S TAKE

Some things you simply don't question because some things are just meant to be. Joining Tyron Woodley's inner circle is both a rare and difficult thing to do. You see, his circle is small for a reason, which makes my relationship with Tyron all the more remarkable.

Most relationships are built over time as you share experiences, earn trust, and reveal inner thoughts. But like so many things about Tyron Woodley that are uncommon, so is how my close relationship with him came to be.

Several years ago, I was contacted by the manager of a local UFC fighter from St. Louis. The manager said this fighter had read my book, *Own YOUR Success,* and since both of us were in St. Louis, that I needed to come down to his gym to meet him. I'm a positive and open person, but normally I can only move so fast when developing a relationship with someone else. It's a give-and-take process, fueled in part by taking cues from the other person, showing interest in their life, and trying to build bridges that will allow both of you to meet on common ground.

I said, "normally." Tyron Woodley is anything but normal. I walked into the gym, not quite knowing what to expect. Any qualms I had quickly disappeared like a puff of smoke in a strong breeze because Tyron Woodley was gracious from the moment I met him. Within five minutes, it was as if we had known each other our whole lives. Everything about our relationship fast-forwarded from that point on.

I'm sure you've had that happen to you. It

doesn't occur often, but when it does, there is a sixth sense, an immediate trust, perhaps even a bit of déjà vu, that allows you to drop your guard. You are immediately at ease. You just know, by some innate sense, that this is a rare moment, a rare relationship.

Looking back, it may have been our common adversities that instantaneously bonded us. Those adversities were remarkably similar, and they ultimately defined the men we have since become. Sitting in that gym, we talked about the importance of family: the ultimate small circle! Our conversation also touched upon mindset and how the right mindset means everything when your goal is greatness.

I walked away that day feeling energized. I fed off of Tyron's positivity and ability to focus, and in return, I helped him to hone his mindset, removing barriers so that he could become the best possible version of himself.

Since that time, we've explored a lot of things, including a few dark places that might leave outsiders questioning our sanity. But exploring those dark places, where fear, anger, and suffering reside, are crucial to fully understanding yourself. You may think of this as uncommon, but I've learned that only by making peace with your demons can you reach your highest levels of performance. When you understand what your demons are and how they work, they lose power over you; they no longer control you. Being honest with yourself is difficult, but it's necessary if you want to move beyond your current limits.

Many people only see the public friendship I have with Tyron: the pictures of us together on the walls of his gym and locker room. They listen to speeches we've given together. But for us, it goes much deeper than that.

We have an "iron sharpens iron" relationship. We both make each other better. That creates a natural gravitation toward each other, a dynamic that has been in operation since the first time we met. I can't explain how or why. As I said, some things just are meant to be, and you must accept them and practice gratitude for those gifts. And there are few things in life I am more grateful for than to be a part of Tyron Woodley's small circle.

8

CHAUNTÉ LOWE

Nobody goes looking for adversity in their lives. However, sooner or later, adversity finds you. It is the nature of our existence. You can't control when, how, or where, but you do have a choice on how you respond. And Chaunté Lowe can show you exactly how to do it.

She has competed in four Olympics and is a four-time medalist in the women's high jump. An eight-time national outdoor champion, she is the American record holder for the women's outdoor high jump at 2.05 meters (6 feet, 8 ¾ inches) and holds the indoor high jump record as well.

Chaunté is also no stranger to adversity. As a child, her mother battled addiction. Her father spent time in prison. She eventually wound up living with her grandmother. Her grandmother took her to church several times a week, and faith became the guiding light that saved her.

Blessed with natural jumping ability, Chaunté bounded her way into a scholarship at Georgia Tech and made her first Olympic team while she was a sophomore. Since that time, her athletic accomplishments have been impressive by any measure, made even more so by the fact that she gave birth to three children along the way. In fact, she won the 2012 world indoor championship less than a year after giving birth to her second daughter.

But it turns out, all of those achievements were just a prelude to Chaunté clearing the biggest hurdle of her life: cancer. And not just any kind of cancer. In June 2019, at age 35, she was diagnosed with triple-negative invasive ductal carcinoma, an aggressive form of breast cancer. Triple-negative cancer means hormone therapy, and targeted drugs don't work to combat the disease. If caught early enough, it's treatable, but even then, options are limited. The regimen is brutal, requiring five months of intensive chemotherapy that destroys every part of your body. In Chaunté's case, it also meant undergoing a double mastectomy.

The treatment wiped her out so much that on many days Chaunté was reduced to using a walker to get around. She spent other times sleeping more than 24 hours straight to try and heal her body. You can't run fast enough or jump high enough to get away from an insidious disease like cancer. In fact, the more you try to outrun cancer, the worse it gets.

Instead, to beat cancer, you have to take on a champion's competitive mentality. You have to embrace the life-challenging adversity of cancer. You have to battle it head-on; there is no other way. And that's exactly what Chaunté did.

How do you cope? How do you mentally prepare? How do you go from being the finest athlete in your sport to having to use a walker to get around while you heal?

Here's how Chaunté did it. First, you accept your situation, then you embrace it.

You don't have a choice about the hand you've been dealt. But you do have a choice as to how you respond, how you choose to fight your situation.

With cancer or any life-threatening disease for that matter, it's easy to become depressed and fight within yourself: to battle between wanting to give up or not.

Or you can fight a completely different way,

as Chaunté did. You enter into attack mode. You align your thoughts, emotions, and your body. And then, when you're in sync, you fight your battle with everything you have.

In that battle, you don't think much about training for your fifth Olympics, which Chaunté was doing when doctors diagnosed her. Instead, you face the immediate adversity that has been set squarely in front of you. You take bigger goals, like getting healthy, and break them down into smaller and more achievable goals, like just being able to walk around the block. You celebrate small victories, slowly rebuilding toward good health as you are able.

When you can embrace adversity, you are better able to beat adversity. Already admired as an accomplished Olympic athlete, as she regained her health, Chaunté shifted gears and used her platform to become a leader in a different kind of cause. As a cancer survivor, she began advocating for testing and early detection of cancer in younger women. Usually, mammograms aren't given to women under 40. But if Chaunté had waited until she was 40 instead of insisting on one after she suspected something was wrong, she probably wouldn't have survived.

By circumstance and adversity, Chaunté has

become a leading advocate of early screening as the best defense against cancer. She also understands that when she trains now, it's not just for her. She has become a role model, a leader in a way nobody, least of all her, could have imagined. By embracing the adversity in her life, Chaunté took something terrible and turned it into something positive.

She also knows the stakes are raised for the next Olympics, too. When Chaunté makes the Olympic team—her fifth, and an extraordinary feat in its own right—she can use her platform to promote a cause that means everything to her.

She has become a leader, but she has also become much more. By embracing her adversity, Chaunté Lowe is saving lives, and there is no more noble cause or better life lived than that.

BEN'S TAKE

I often speak about process, mindset, and overcoming adversity. For some people, that means shaving a few seconds off your personal best time running a mile. For others, it's sharpening your focus and your efforts to give you the edge you need to win an important game or land a huge piece of business for your company. I work with people every day who are engaged in personal challenges, overcoming obstacles, and digging deep to achieve their personal bests. Their challenges and their goals are personal and real.

For Chaunté Lowe, setting goals and overcoming challenges have always been a big part of her life. But what makes Chaunté different, what makes her leadership more uncommon than most everyone else I know, is the ultimate challenge of winning life over death.

I've met many remarkable women over the years: Teri Griege, an ironwoman triathlete who completed the Kona Ironman in Hawaii while suffering from stage 4 cancer; my mother's caregiver, Carolyn Harris, who was a beacon of strength and kindness for my brother and me during our most troubling times; and my wife, Ami, who came from the rural confines of Edinburg, Illinois, and rose to become a top-level executive at Anheuser-Busch. There are so many more.

What I know for sure is that my list would not be complete without Chaunté Lowe. I was already familiar with her story when I shared the stage with Chaunté in Orlando a few years ago. But I never fully appreciated her resilience and ability to overcome the harshest of setbacks until that day.

Fighting cancer is often a private battle, and an extra layer of energy is required if you are a public figure: a layer that can sap your focus and drain your stamina. When you're fighting cancer, those distractions can make the difference between surviving or not.

Somehow, Chaunté defied the odds and was able to muster the next level of strength. She turned the tables and used her struggle to become a role model for what it means to attack life's greatest challenge when the stakes can't possibly be higher.

Life doesn't always treat us fairly. It's easy to give up when things don't go our way. But not until you are backed into a corner can you fully understand how much fight there is in you.

When she asked me to be a part of Team Lowe to help her prep to compete in her fifth Olympics, it was among the most sacred of all honors and an opportunity I will cherish for the rest of my life. I've been blessed to get to know Chaunté and often think of her when I'm facing my own challenges or when I'm working with others to overcome their battles.

There are no guarantees in life. You may win, and you may not. That's why, to fight your best fight *is* to win—that is the real victory.

You can't always control the outcome, but you can control the process. In fact, it's the only thing you can control.

By living her best life in the face of the grave odds stacked against her, Chaunté remains an uncommon leader and someone I am proud to count as one of my most inspirational friends.

9

JERRY RICE

HOW CAN SOMEBODY NOT GIVE 100 PERCENT WHEN IT'S 100 PERCENT THEIR CHOICE?

J erry Rice is the best wide receiver ever to play professional football. By any measure, there's no room for argument: Jerry holds 36 NFL records, including scoring 208 touchdowns, the most in NFL history; Emmitt Smith is a distant second, with 175 career TDs. He also owns virtually every significant wide receiver record, including 1,549 receptions, 22,895 receiving yards, and 274 consecutive games with at least one catch, among many others. Jerry was also an integral part of three Super Bowl champion teams along the way.

When you are this successful in your profession, it's pretty much a given that others will seek you out, looking for even the tiniest of insights and wisdom they can use in their own lives. Jerry is no exception. He has been quoted thousands of times during his career, so if you're looking for insights from Jerry, it's hard to pick out one that stands head and shoulders above the rest. But for my money, no quote sums up Jerry's key to success better than this one:

Today I will do what others won't, so tomorrow I can accomplish what others can't.

Simple, yet profound, it captures Jerry's championship mindset, on and off the field. This has been Jerry's game plan for life.

His actions are intentional. There was nothing random about how Jerry approached football during his playing days or how he approaches life now. Jerry's level of success didn't happen by accident. It required hard work, sweat, determination, sacrifice, and focus—for years and years at a time.

If you want to enjoy even a fraction of the success Jerry has enjoyed, you can't give 99 percent; you must give 100 percent—all of the time.

Jerry credits his success in part to his "All the Time Mindset," which means you do things only one way, all the time. Your approach to off-season training, in-season practices, and game-day prep are no different than when you step on the field for a game on Sunday. Performing at 100 percent becomes second nature because that's all you do. In fact, it's all you know how to do, every moment of every day, all the time.

Some will argue people are born this way. Others make the case that it is a function of developing self-discipline and an undeniable mindset. In Jerry's case, the will to succeed blossomed out of not wanting to disappoint his parents. He openly points out that they were the guiding forces who instilled in him the desire to perform at the highest levels at all times. That's not bad for a kid who didn't even start playing football—somewhat by fluke—until his sophomore year in high school.

Jerry was trying to dodge class one day when he inadvertently ran into an assistant principal, did an about-face, and sprinted down the hall to avoid punishment. Jerry's speed caught the assistant principal's eye, which quickly turned into a recommendation to the school's football coach. He fully immersed himself in football and would go on to earn top high school honors by being named All-State in Mississippi. Mississippi Valley State University recruited Jerry, where he broke NCAA records for receptions, yards, and touchdowns. Jerry also earned the nickname

"World," because there wasn't a ball in the world he couldn't catch.

Because he loved and respected the game, Jerry also respected the process of what it takes to play the game well—extraordinarily well. The old adage of "when you love what you do, you'll never work a day in your life" could not ring truer in Jerry's case. His single-minded dedication to perfecting his craft is legendary.

For the first ten years he was in the league, Jerry and his wife never took a vacation. Together, they chose to focus on Jerry's career as an NFL wide receiver instead. In fact, Jerry chose the path of giving 100 percent throughout his entire football career. It's a philosophy that stayed with him until the final snap of the final game he played.

Consider another quote from Jerry that reveals how driven he was:

I was always in search of a perfect game, and I never got it.

Think about that. With all of his accomplishments, Jerry was still aiming to be better to the end of his career. His "unfinished business" was an elusive goal that amplified his desire to always give 100 percent. It brought added focus to his efforts. He used this goal as motivation to keep performing at the highest possible level.

The question then becomes, "What does this have to do with leadership?" It's simple. Through his dedication and exemplary work ethic, Jerry leads by example. This, despite the fact by his own admission, Jerry is a naturally reserved and quiet man.

It may sound a bit cliché, but actions do speak louder than words. In Jerry's case, giving 100 percent as a way of life is an actionable choice. On the other hand, you could also argue it's not even a choice for Jerry. This way of thinking has become so ingrained in his mind that there is no other way to live his life.

However, for you, it is a choice, and that choice is this: Given the option of attacking your life's challenges with 100 percent instead of less than 100 percent, why would you settle for anything less?

BEN'S TAKE

I watched his games. I consumed books, articles, television shows, and online videos about him. I studied his life, wanting to know how Jerry Rice became the greatest wide receiver ever to play professional football. I thought I had a strong sense of who he was and what made him so great.

But it wasn't until I found myself standing next to Jerry backstage at one of our Boot Camps in 2016 that I truly understood the uncommon commitment and belief he had in "the process." We engaged in some small talk, swapped stories about preparation, discipline, and dedication to your craft. And then I simply asked him, "What is it that makes you so great?" I'm sure he had been asked that question thousands of times over, as have many high achievers. But the answer I got was not the answer I was expecting.

Jerry answered my question with a question of his own. "You know what I've never understood? How could somebody not give 100 percent, when it's 100 percent their choice?" It was an "a-ha" moment that will stay with me for the rest of my life.

No need to overcomplicate things; the thinking is simple and pure. If you're looking for an uncommon approach to leadership, all you have to do, in Jerry's case, is flip the script: most people struggle to give 100 percent, but Jerry doesn't know anything else.

There's a wide chasm between good enough and being great. Consider this. When your process is defined by a mindset that giving 100 percent is all there is, the process is simplified. By removing the option of less than 100 percent, you don't need to worry that you gave your process 95 percent, or 80 percent, or whatever number it is you feel comfortable with. No matter what else happens in your life, when you live to that standard, you build a hard defense against letting your feelings or other outside forces detract from your focus and determination. It is the difference between what you do and who you are.

There are so many talented athletes, musicians, writers, business people, doctors, philosophers, and those of many other occupations in this world. But to be the best of the best in your field, what you do must become who you are. There can be no difference; your identity and your results are intertwined with who you are.

So, when the name "Jerry Rice" is mentioned, you don't think of him as just a great wide receiver because that's what he did. You think of him as the greatest wide receiver to ever play the game because that's who he is.

Some will say to achieve this level of greatness requires sacrifice. I don't believe that. If you are that laser-focused on what you do and you live and love the pursuit of achieving the highest level of performance that you can, there is no sacrifice. There is only inner peace, knowing you have accepted the ultimate challenge of your life and done everything you can to meet the goals you have set for yourself. Many people aspire to this level, but only a few have the sustained mental toughness and required long-term dedication it takes to be the greatest at whatever you choose to do with your life.

If you're looking for an uncommon leader with a blueprint you can adopt, start with Jerry Rice. And be ready to commit to 100 percent as a lifelong standard.

INTENTIONAL FOCUS

NOBODY BREAKS YOUR FOCUS. What YOU see NOW will happen IN THE FUTURE. VISUALIZE and prepare and the race will slow down for YOU. Use INTENTIONAL FOCUS in all areas of the daily PROCESS.

LOCK IN to YOUR ideal state of FOCUS. LEAD and BE YOU one day at a time. Take action with your team and EXECUTE.

Focus on ACTIONS versus the PRESSURE created by other individuals' attention to the results, the things they can't control. Pressure causes YOU to look ahead. Pressure causes YOU to feel defeated in anticipation of what may happen. That is not how winning is done.

VS. PRESSURE

10.

DAVID GOGGINS

THE UNCOMMON AMONG THE UNCOMMON

After you get to know his story, one of the easiest things you'll ever be asked to do is describe David Goggins's life in one word. That word is "extreme."

There is nothing subtle about David; there has never been. He is the uncommon man who walks among common people.

You've undoubtedly heard of the path of least resistance. David chooses to lead a life on the path of most resistance. He is comfortable being very uncomfortable, because in David's mind, the only way you gain mental toughness is to do things you're not happy doing. That's where the most growth occurs. He believes you must be in a constant state of positive growth and change. You are either getting better or getting worse, but you are never staying the same.

David's life has been anything but average. As a young child, he worked in his father's bowling alley in Buffalo, New York, rarely attending school because his father didn't value education. He worked late many evenings and slept on an office couch until his mother got off at 3:00 a.m. from working in his father's adjoining bar. That's extreme.

When he was still a young child, his mother left his father and took David and his brother to live in a small town in Indiana. Unfortunately, David's family was one of the very few Black families in a town that still had an active Ku Klux Klan chapter. You can guess what the family endured in the years that followed. Also extreme.

When you grow up in an extreme environment, you tend to think extreme thoughts. Those thoughts can often go to a dark place, and it's tough to blame someone who ends up there. But that wasn't the case with David.

After a stint in the Air Force, he became a pest exterminator, and his weight ballooned. David carried that weight like baggage packed with all the negative energy in his life up to that point.

He was at a crossroads: mediocrity or an amazing life? David chose the latter—in an extreme way, of course.

He set his sights on rejoining the military, and not just any branch, mind you, but the US Navy SEALs. There was one jumbo problem, though: the SEALs don't take guys who weigh 280 pounds, which is where David was, due to heavy weight training. So, David flipped a switch.

He started building and crystallizing an "uncommon mindset." By definition, an uncommon mindset means taking your mind to a place where others aren't willing to go. You rise above to an uncommon place, define exactly how much you're willing to do to achieve challenging goals, and throw everything you have at your efforts— every single day.

In David's case, an uncommon mindset meant taking whatever steps were necessary to become a US Navy Seal. He went on a diet and exercise regimen that defied description. Over the next 60 days, he lost 100 pounds.

That is not a typo. It is extreme, and an example of the power of an uncommon mindset.

But David didn't stop there. Motivated by the horrific loss of life in the special ops ranks in Afghanistan, including many guys he had trained with, David set his sights on raising money and awareness for fallen and severely wounded soldiers through the Special Operations Warrior Project. To draw attention to his cause, David focused his military service to become one of the best endurance athletes on the planet. He became the *only* member of the US Armed Forces ever to complete SEAL training, US Army Ranger School, and Air Force Tactical Air Controller training.

He became a Guinness World Record holder by completing 4,030 pull-ups in 17 hours. David has also competed in more than 60 ultra-marathons, triathlons, and ultra-triathlons, setting many new course records and regularly placing among the top finishers.

Those are extreme to begin with, but one story illustrates how David's Uncommon Mindset took him one step beyond.

Jesse Itzler, the Atlanta Hawks owner, ran as part of a relay in a 100-mile race. David also ran in the same race, but he ran the entire 100 miles *solo*. David broke all the small bones in his feet and had kidney failure during the race. Itzler, both inspired and curious, sought him out, wanting to tap into that same vein of mental toughness. David spent the next month living with Itzler and his wife, teaching the couple how best to achieve their version of an uncommon mindset.

Word of feats like David's does get around. You become a leader when you are thrust into the spotlight by your accomplishments. Like David, you're not required to think any certain way when it comes to deciding how to live your life. You're not required to challenge yourself daily to be the best that you can. It is a choice.

Let me repeat that: an uncommon mindset is a choice. It means making a total commitment to yourself so that your mental toughness can produce otherwise unimaginable results for you. Then you become a leader by attracting attention through your actions.

David retired from the SEALs, but he has not lost his passion for meeting new goals. He has become a highly sought-after motivational speaker for Fortune 500 companies, pro sports teams, and thousands of students worldwide.

He also published a book in late 2018. *Can't Hurt Me: Master Your Mind and Defy the Odds* reveals his life story and introduces the 40% Rule that explains how most of us only tap into 40 percent of our capabilities. This is a must-read textbook on how to push past your pain to reach your full potential.

As of late 2020, it has been on the *New York*

Times Bestseller list for 96 weeks (and even longer by the time you read this). It has also repeatedly been recognized by Amazon as one of the Top 20 Most Sold & Most Read Books of the Week. It has received rave reviews from thousands of readers. In other words, the book has been *extremely* successful—of course it has. And now that you know more about David's story, you shouldn't be surprised by this.

BEN'S TAKE

I haven't spent much time with David Goggins. But that does not mean he hasn't had a significant impact on me and the way I think.

We crossed paths briefly at my first Coach Saban–University of Alabama training camp in 2018. Tuscaloosa in August is sweltering, but you're there for a reason. The coaches, the team, David, and I had work to do. We were both on the sidelines during a Saturday practice when I exchanged glances with David.

You know a man is intense when a simple exchange of glances is memorable. What I saw on that face was the most locked-in, fired-up person I've ever run across. I introduced myself, we shook hands, and I could tell instantly this was an uncommon man. Although we only chatted briefly, what struck me the most about him was his focus and how much he believed in himself.

David just carries himself differently from other high achievers I've met. It wasn't what he said as much as how he said it when we talked. I knew he was tough and that he had accomplished a lot in his life. But standing there with him, I could see the look in his eyes and how he refused to accept anything remotely associated with failure.

As you might guess, his session later that evening had the desired effect on the team. But our meeting also had a desired effect on me. I was transfixed by what I heard and saw. I knew I had to find out more about David. My natural curiosity kicked in.

Where did he come from? What was his story? How did he become the person I saw and talked to that day?

So, I studied him. I watched and read everything there was to know about him. But what really locked me in was his book. I pored over *Can't Hurt Me*; to say that it resonated is an understatement.

I've revisited that book several times. David's clarity of purpose and his philosophy continues to influence me to this day. In fact, David Goggins's mindset has become my mindset—because it works. I believe in the concept of the uncommon mindset, so much so that I created a similar way of thinking that I call the "unrequired mindset."

Be forewarned if you also decide to read his book; David uses a lot of "colorful" language that will be off-putting to some people. George Carlin called these types of words "intensifiers," and since David is the most intense man on the planet, using these words is very much in character for him. It's an honest way to convey his version of how to succeed. It's raw, and it's honest, and that is David, through and through.

I like to think of his approach as intentional intensity. Or, as David likes to say, "There are no excuses in life, only reasons to try harder."

11.

JANET FISHMAN NEWMAN

IT'S NOT HOW LONG YOU LIVE, IT'S HOW YOU CHOOSE TO LIVE YOUR LIFE—LEAVE YOUR LEGACY

Janet Fishman Newman was my mother. She died eleven days before my eighth birthday, and she was only 38 years old.

Although I miss her every single day, I don't dwell upon her death. Instead, I celebrate how she lived her life. I didn't have a choice of how long she lived; it was God's will and beyond my control. But I do have a choice as to how I remember her.

Her passing is an ongoing reminder to me that we control very few things in our lives. We are guaranteed nothing. Some things are forced upon us, but in large part, our lives are defined by the choices we make until we draw our last breath. How we choose to face adversity says as much about us while we are here as it does when we ultimately pass on. That's why the most valuable lesson in leadership is the lesson I learned from my mother.

She suffered from amyloidosis. It's a rare disease that causes amyloid protein to build up in body organs. When this happens, these organs start to fail, leading to a series of debilitating symptoms. There is no cure. Treatment can alleviate some symptoms temporarily, but ultimately the disease will win. That was the case with my mother. She battled bravely for four hard years before succumbing.

What I didn't know at the time is that my mother had created a journal about her experiences while she was sick. My grandmother kept it tucked away until I was in college. When she gave it to me, I couldn't get past the first page and had to set it aside until I was more ready to read it, which wasn't for several more years.

The journal was more than a chronicle of my mother's fight against amyloidosis; it was a bounty of her accumulated wisdom. This was more than just a personal message to me and my brother. It contained universal wisdom, wisdom that needed to be shared. In life, my mother was a teacher by profession. But even after her passing, she remained a teacher. Through my mother's recorded thoughts and words, I still learn from her every day.

Above all else, when faced with the inevitable, my mother taught me that our life's circumstances are much less significant than our responses to them. It's not how long you live; it's how you live your life while you are here.

You only have a small say in how long you'll live. But you have an almost unlimited ability to choose how you will live while you are alive. You can choose passivity, or you can choose to be an active participant in your own life. You can choose to be a victim, or you can choose to fight and do whatever you can to overcome obstacles in your life.

Passive people are followers; fighters are leaders. When you make a conscious choice to be a fighter and lead others with your wisdom, knowledge, and compassion, you will positively impact them, sometimes forever.

Remember this: whether you are a father, mother, sibling, boss, co-worker, neighbor, elected official, teacher, or whatever labels you wear in life, be conscious of the fact that you will leave a legacy. It is up to you to decide whether or not it will be a positive and enduring legacy.

Unfortunately, the sad fact is that some people

choose to ignore this responsibility. They choose to be selfish, self-absorbed, and greedy with their time, thoughts, and good fortunes. You can't control these people. You can only control elements of your life that God has given to you as part of your free will.

If you are not living the way you want to live, you must change the way you think before changing the way you live. Indeed, what you do with the gift of free will is up to you.

Even as she suffered, my mother could have given up. But she understood her responsibility. She embraced her role as a mother, as a teacher. Even when she was sick, my mother was the greatest champion of life I have ever known. She knew that even though her days were short, her legacy could be everlasting. Despite her pain, she led me to a better place.

Do I wish I could have spent more time with her before she passed? Yes, of course. But when I think about it and honor her by living my life in the ways she continues to teach me, I am spending time with her. I am her legacy.

BEN'S TAKE

Some people lead thousands, or even millions of others, daily. Think of the CEO of a Fortune 500 company or the President of the United States. Each has the power to impact countless lives through their thoughts and actions.

But some leaders directly impact only one or two people. Suppose those people are intimately woven into your life. In that case, their lessons and their leadership can have a more profound and lasting impact than any corporate or government persona you will ever encounter.

Fortunately, I have been blessed to learn from so many wise and thoughtful leaders in my life. I've applied those lessons, tried to be a good steward of that knowledge, and endeavored to pass it along to you.

Some of those people are in this book. And while they all matter, there has been no greater teacher, no greater mentor, than my mother. While she touched many lives in her thirty-eight short years on this earth, the two lives she impacted the most were my brother, Drew, and me.

Many people are fortunate to have someone they can look up to in their lives. Those who influence you may never run big companies, lead troops into battle, or govern the masses. But they will have a direct impact on your life, which matters in a supreme way. Because every life is unique, their leadership lessons will be unique. Although many leaders share the same value systems, you will see their influence as uncommon in a one-on-one relationship because their lessons directly impact you in a way unlike anyone else.

Such was the case with my mother. Despite a fatal diagnosis of amyloidosis, my mother never wavered in her love for us. Once she set her mind to it, she overcame tremendous pain and set a personal standard of remaining involved in our lives for as long as she could.

It would have been so easy to cave into the disease. After all, although you can treat symptoms, ultimately amyloidosis will win. My mother knew this.

But if one of the defining characteristics of uncommon leadership is courage, then my mother had it in abundance. Her purpose connected her to a wellspring of courage.

I have written extensively about her struggles. I think about her often. As the years go by, the lessons she taught me to grow in meaning and importance. They have shaped me and have helped me shape countless others.

The lesson for you is this: never underestimate your ability to be a leader, even if it only means being a good dad, mom, sibling, grandparent, or friend. You may only impact or lead a single person. However, we are all connected on this planet, and the seed you plant could travel far, with untold impacts to bloom and affect others. You may not see it as a responsibility to lead others positively, but it is. View it as a gift, if you must.

The gift my mother gave me has taken me to so many places and given me purpose and direction to help others; her ripple effect is profound.

Like me, you can draw strength from the leaders in your life to keep the fire lit that produces the burn inside of you. Similarly, you can light the fire that creates the burn inside anyone you come in contact with, even if it is only one or two people.

My mother understood this. She understood her legacy. She not only accepted the limitations that life had placed upon her—she embraced and made the most of those limitations. My mother set an example and taught me that there is no lesson too small to learn, that there is no life so young or insignificant that you can't have a positive impact on it.

Be mindful of each person in your life; be mindful of how you can lead them by your thoughts and your actions. Be an uncommon leader, and I guarantee that you will live a very good life.

Just like my mother, Janet Fishman Newman.

WHAT IS **THE BURN**?

Oftentimes we only hear about the accolades of someone great (awards received, championships won, etc).

I have found over the last 14+ years of working with some of the world's top performers in business and sports that there is something that DRIVES them to that greatness...and it goes deeper than just their WHY or PURPOSE.

The BURN is what really lights them up to believe anything is possible. It's the mindset that causes them to fight on a different level. That same BURN lies inside of YOU. It lights YOUR why on fire and drives YOU to take the necessary actions.

The BURN in your heart, that underlying passion will help YOU fight through anything in your life and emerge on a different plane than that of where YOU started.

The BURN Challenge: Think about how often you have connected with your BURN the last 30 days. If it hasn't been consistent enough, why not start NOW and connect to it today?

Stay locked in on that purpose and do it again every single day from here on out, granting yourself the opportunity to achieve like you never have before.

Connect deeper to the BURN that lies inside of you that will drive YOUR greatest levels of performance.

@CONTINUEDFIGHT

MORE BOOKS BY BEN

Leave Your Legacy

Learn to live a truly exceptional life with the help of author, speaker, and performance coach Ben Newman. In *Leave YOUR Legacy*, you will see firsthand how to drive impact by changing your perspective and connecting to your life's purpose.

Newman shows you how to be your best self with this touching story that clearly illuminates the steps needed to create major change in your life by following the ups and downs of the protagonist, Pierce. Join Pierce on his journey to greatness—from the humble beginnings of enacting change and resisting old behaviors to the reframing of his thoughts and actions and eventually understanding his legacy.

Experience for yourself the ripple effect of leaving YOUR legacy. Pierce's story will inspire you to go do great things. And, as you strive for excellence, you will inspire excellence in others. Are you ready to unleash your full potential? It's time to uncover your drive, your passion, and your purpose—leave YOUR legacy.

"Own Your Success connects you to your life's purpose. *Leave YOUR Legacy* will redefine your thinking to embrace change and leave an impact on others."

—Will Compton

NFL Linebacker, Former Washington Redskins Defensive Captain

Own YOUR Success

National Bestseller and named by CEO Read
as their #13 Business Book of 2012!

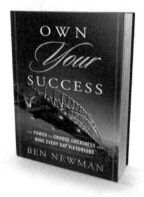

What if you could make each and every day victorious by focusing on daily activities rather than obsessing over results that you can't control? Based on author Ben Newman's popular program, *Own YOUR Success* gives you the power to make each day a triumph. The most successful people find great success when they focus on having a passion for the process. The key: make today victorious regardless of the obstacles that come your way. Figure out what fires YOU up without exception and ignite that passion so that you can routinely create your prizefighter day.

Own YOUR Success will lead you to uncover your true potential and create a life that belongs to YOU.

"I firmly believe that we are where we are in life because of our choices. Being great is also a choice and it helps if there are resources that would help us understand the process that causes one to be great. Well now you have it! *Own Your Success* is one of those resources. Read it and it will help you release your potential."

—Aeneas Williams
NFL Hall-of-Fame Cornerback
14 year NFL Veteran and 8 time Pro-bowler

YOUR Mental Toughness Playbook

National Bestseller and named by CEO Read as their #13 Business Book of 2012!

Are you ready for the next level of YOUR success?

One of the first rules of sport psychology is for an athlete to perform at their highest level. They can't solely rely on their natural talents and abilities; they must understand the mental toughness side of what it takes to achieve peak performance.

Ben believes this is the same in anyone's life. This does not just apply to athletes, it applies to teachers, Fortune 500 executives, salespeople, professionals, those leading others in business and life. This concept applies to all individuals fighting to achieve peak performance in their lives.

This playbook and video series is about YOUR mental toughness and embracing the fact that your success is not just about changing your habits; it's about changing the way that you think. The most successful people are those who exemplify the importance of combining great habits and passion for the process with their ability to embrace adversity and challenge—to remain strong in driving their goals to completion.

In this program, we will explore six phases of YOUR Mental Toughness. The phases include Attaining Belief in Yourself, The Power to REFRAME, YOUR "I AM" statements, YOUR Prizefighter Day, YOUR Legacy Statement, and creating YOUR Environment for Greatness.

This is YOUR opportunity to drive more significant results in YOUR life by coupling the mental toughness side of what it takes to achieve peak performance with YOUR natural talents and abilities to serve others and make a difference in the world.

———

"The energy and enthusiasm for life in the room was off the charts during Ben's presentation. The LEGACY and mental toughness message that was delivered inspired all of us to strive for our potential as we prepare together for the next chapter of our Creighton Basketball program."

—Steve Merfeld

Creighton Men's Basketball Assistant Head Coach

Fight the Good Fight

Fight the Good Fight provides inspiration for individuals who choose to embrace adversity in order to reach success. Over twenty years ago Ben Newman suffered the loss of his mother after years of watching her health deteriorate. After her tragic passing, his grandmother gave him an unexpected gift, in the form of a journal his mother left behind . . . A journey that is poignant, emotional, and sometimes heartbreaking, this is a story that you will remember forever in your soul.

"Fight the Good Fight is one of those quick reads that I had trouble putting down. The heart gets involved as Ben Newman exposes his own, with the tragedies that motivated him to help others. The idea of persistence, and legacy are right on track with every successful athlete and business man I know, and the insights in this book will hit the competitor in each of us, right between the eyes."

—**Mike Matheny**
Manager of the Kansas City Royals

Pocket Truths for Success

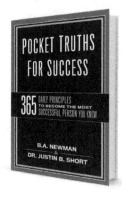

Pocket Truths for Success is your succinct guide to establishing priorities and achieving success in life. Pocket Truths for Success was written to be an inspiration for anyone facing the seemingly insurmountable challenges on the road to life's great successes. Personally and professionally, success is a difficult endeavor and possibly even harder to sustain once achieved. This book was written to address the two pivotal issues of achieving and sustaining success, in the complex ever-changing world we live in today. *Pocket Truths* delivers simple and powerful quotes for those ready to inspire and lead.

"Pocket Truths will inspire you to lead yourself, to lead others, and to make positive waves of change in the future. This book will concisely enable you to define your LEGACY!"

—Jon Gordon

New York Times **Bestseller of "The Energy Bus"**

BE EMPOWERED TO BE UNCOMMON

Ben Newman speaks to conventions, organizations and teams all over the world. The Ben Newman Companies, a professional speaking and consulting company, conducts boot camps, seminars and in-depth training in the areas of mental toughness, high performance sales, teamwork, leadership, and relationship building.

————————

Ben's customized speaking and coaching leaves audiences inspired, educated, AND empowered! Participants are able to uncover their true potential, readying them to create the life they are meant to fight for and enjoy. Emerging poised to take on THEIR relentless pursuit of greatness: Their Prizefighter day!

————————

If you are interested in purpose driven programs through THE UNCOMMON COACHING PROGRAM, based upon the principles of "Uncommon Leadership," contact The Ben Newman Companies at info@BenNewman.net.

STAY CONNECTED

---

f *Ben Newman*

🐦 *@Continued Fight*

📷 *@Continued Fight*

in *Ben Newman*

▶ *Ben Newman | The Burn*

LEARN MORE AT
WWW.BENNEWMAN.NET

ABOUT THE AUTHOR

Ben Newman is a highly regarded performance coach, international speaker, and
best-selling author whose clients include Fortune 500 companies around the world, business
executives, sales organizations, and athletes in the
NFL, PGA, NBA, MLB, UFC, and NCAA.

Ben serves as a mental conditioning coach

for the 18-time National Champion Alabama Crimson Tide football team and has worked with players from the last three Super Bowl Champion teams. He was recently selected by Influencive. com as one of the Top 10 Motivators in Sports, and *Real Leaders Magazine* selected him as one of their 2019 and 2020 Top 50 Speakers in the World.

In 2021 Ben's highly anticipated new book *Uncommon Leadership* will be released. Despite the adversities of COVID-19, the BNC Speakers group and BNC Coaching group have had a tremendous impact on organizations, helping them finding alternative ways to drive growth.

His clients have included: Microsoft, United States Army, Anheuser-Busch InBev, Quicken Loans, Miami Dolphins, MARS Snackfoods, Kansas State Football, St. Louis Cardinals, North Dakota State Bison Football, Northwestern Mutual, AFA Singapore, Mass Financial Group, Wells Fargo Advisors, Great West Life Canada, Boston Medical Center, Boys & Girls Club of America, St. Croix, Missouri Tigers Basketball, New York Life, The University of Iowa and The Minnesota Vikings . . . as well as thousands of executives, entrepreneurs, athletes, and sales teams from around the globe.

Ben's authentic, powerful, and engaging storytelling has become internationally recognized, and he has shared the stage with Jerry Rice, Ray Lewis, Tony Dungy, Colin Powell, Brian Tracy, Ken Blanchard, Jon Gordon, Dr. Jason Selk, Floyd Little, Aeneas Williams, Walt Jocketty, and other leaders and legends in the world.

Ben is also the founder of BNC Coaching, BNC Speakers, The Financial Advisor Academy, and The Uncommon Coaching program.

Ben lives in his hometown of St. Louis, Missouri, with the true measure of his success: his wife, Ami, and their children, J. Isaac and Kennedy Rose.

Ben Newman
The Ben Newman Companies
www.BenNewman.net

ACKNOWLEDGMENTS

Books are not written alone, and the highest levels of SUCCESS are always achieved with a great TEAM. Along this journey, many people have been tremendously supportive advocates.

To my greatest team who makes all of this possible, my family: Ami, J. Isaac, and Kennedy Rose. I love you more than words can express.

I would also like to acknowledge our Director of Operations, Anna Jones, our Creative Director, Tyler Kirk, and our President of BNC Coaching, Jeremy Patty. Your daily commitment to greatness helps us continue to fight and impact the thousands of lives we touch each year.

Bret Colson, my esteemed editor: you are truly

incredible. I can't thank you enough for who you are and what you do. Your commitment, passion, eagle eye, writing, and attention to detail have made *Uncommon Leadership* what it is today.

Ed Mylett, thank YOU for your example and how YOU inspire me with the manner in which YOU walk your walk in life. Tremendously grateful for your foreword and capturing the essence of the book.

Additionally, the opportunity to inspire and empower others through my writing would not be possible without the stories told throughout the book and the impact made on my life by Dr. Jason Selk, Jon Gordon, Laura Pierz, Drew Hanlen, Todd Basler, Dr. Edward M. Johnson Jr., Ladue Basketball, Aeneas Williams, Will Compton, Mark Daly, Andy Kaiser, Josh Qualy, Brian Cohen, Michael Kennedy Jr., John Doty, Coach Chris Klieman, Kansas State Football, North Dakota State Football, Coach Nick Saban, Ginger Gilmore, Jeff Allen, Alabama Football, Andy Frisella, Tyron Woodley, Chaunté Lowe, Jerry Rice, and David Goggins. And to each of our clients in the world of sports and business, we are blessed to partner with every day: thank you. We are stronger together, and you are appreciated. Iron sharpens Iron.

A special thank you to my father, Burt Newman, for your lessons of courage and perseverance, along with countless other family and friends who inspire me to keep fighting. I would also like to thank my brother, Drew Newman, my sister, Sophie Newman, and Carolyn Harris.

To my mother, Janet Fishman Newman: you continue to inspire me every day to be the best I can be. You taught me life's greatest lesson of LEGACY, to cherish every day . . . Because it is not how long you live, but how you choose to live your life! The BURN will never go out.

To purchase bulk copies of any of Ben's books at a discount for large groups or your organization, please contact info@BenNewman.net